Heading West

An Interdisciplinary Unit on the American Frontier

Wendy S. Wilson & Jack Papadonis

J. WESTON WALCH PUBLISHER

PORTLAND, MAINE

User's Guide
to
Walch Reproducible Books

As part of our general effort to provide educational materials which are as practical and economical as possible, we have designated this publication a "reproducible book." The designation means that purchase of the book includes purchase of the right to limited reproduction of all pages on which this symbol appears:

Here is the basic Walch policy: We grant to individual purchasers of this book the right to make sufficient copies of reproducible pages for use by all students of a single teacher. This permission is limited to a single teacher, and does not apply to entire schools or school systems, so institutions purchasing the book should pass the permission on to a single teacher. Copying of the book or its parts for resale is prohibited.

Any questions regarding this policy or requests to purchase further reproduction rights should be addressed to:

Permissions Editor
J. Weston Walch, Publisher
321 Valley Street • P. O. Box 658
Portland, Maine 04104-0658

ISBN 0-8251-2909-5

Table of Contents

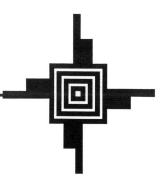

UNIT 3.
Finding a Route

UNIT 4.
Moving West: Wheels, Sails, Hooves, and Rails

UNIT 5.
Selling the West: The Lure of Land and Truth in Advertising

To the Teacher

Exploring the "New Western History"

Over 100 years ago, the historian Frederick Jackson Turner read a paper to the American Historical Association titled "The Significance of the Frontier in American History." Turner's thesis was that Americans were influenced by our nation's unique environment more than they were by the culture of their original homeland. That unique environment, Turner believed, was the frontier—an area of cheap land that drew people predominantly westward. As settlers moved into the "virgin land" away from their old civilization, they discarded many of the customs and restraints that were part of the culture of the more populated and more established areas. They then developed institutions and cultural standards of their own, more suited to their remote settlements in the wilderness. Eventually, as these frontier areas became more populated, settlers adopted or copied the culture of the established areas, but in doing so they discarded any customs or institutions that were not suited to their environment. Thus they created a uniquely "American" society and culture. According to Turner, "The existence of an area of free land, its continuous recession, and the advance of American settlement westward explain American development."

Turner's "Frontier Thesis" has been debated, criticized, and redefined since he first offered it in 1893, but most historians would agree that the westward expansion of this nation and the movement of people into areas of open land not restricted by European notions of land tenure was a significant part of the story of the United States. The frontier, which moved from east to west throughout the history of the nation's settlement, has become a land of myth and legend, an area that makes up a unique part of our cultural heritage, from Johnny Appleseed to Laura Ingalls Wilder to Buffalo Bill Cody and Chief Sitting Bull.

All humans living in the North and South American continents are descendants of immigrants. Even the Native Americans probably crossed the Bering Strait land bridge from Asia thousands of years ago. As the new arrivals came to America, they brought with them a richness and diversity that are still evident in America today. Yet, there is also a unique American culture that continues to bind us as a people—an appreciation for our past history, an interest in our antecedents. This is demonstrated by the increasing popularity of living history museums and reenactments of historical events. Whether it is Sturbridge Village in Massachusetts, the Amana Colonies in Iowa, the Stuhr Museum of the Prairie Pioneer in

Nebraska, or the Mission of San Juan Capistrano in California, Americans flock to these attractions to regain a sense of past and community. Popular films such as *Dances with Wolves* and documentaries such as *The West* by Ken Burns and Stephen Ives reflect this interest in the past.

The United States has always been a balancing act between cultures brought from abroad and a new culture that developed in an environmentally unique land. As people headed west in their quest for new opportunities, they brought few personal possessions but much in the way of knowledge and culture. Their experiences in the freedom of the vast new lands helped to form and change their lifestyles and attitudes and contributed to our distinctive national identity. This identity embraces individualism and diversity, yet also recognizes a sense of a common past heritage in pursuing the "American dream" of open opportunity for economic, social, and political advancement in an environment of freedom. The immigrant experience is a part of all our lives.

This reproducible book is designed to give students an opportunity to investigate different aspects of the westward movement in an interdisciplinary study. The history of the western expansion is currently undergoing some dramatic new revisions. This reproducible book is an attempt to incorporate the new western scholarship into our schools. We have not attempted to tell the entire story of the westward expansion. For example, we do not cover the conflict between the settlers and the Native Americans because of the many materials already available on this topic.

The units that we do provide have many cross-curricular threads and have relevance for our current social studies standards. We encourage you to pick and choose units and topics of interest to you from among all those offered here. Each unit is a suitable stand-alone lesson. Included within each unit are activities of varying sophistication and reading level. The teacher's guide to each unit explains the activities and their level of difficulty, which will help you individualize within classes or course levels. In addition to the units, the book includes six "A Page from the Past" handouts that you can use as high-interest enrichment readings. Unit 7 contains an alternative assessment activity that you could use as a culminating activity for the entire book. The last unit examines using the Internet to research the westward expansion. Concluding materials include an annotated bibliography of resources for teachers and students, a collection of additional assessment activities, and an answer key for appropriate worksheets.

In dealing with the history of the westward movement of the American people, it is important for teachers to realize that this topic is one of controversy and revision. Historians today feel that the story of the West as told in the past passed over such issues as the ecological devastation caused by the pioneers; the role of the Spanish in western culture; the contribution of women, African Americans, and Asians to the development of the West; and the destruction of the Native Americans and the forcible possession of their ancestral lands. We have provided resources in the Bibliography that will help you deal with these issues.

It is also important to remember that at one time, every location in America was a frontier for a group of newcomers—whether they were the first Native Americans as they moved from Siberia down through the North and South American continents, the Pilgrims landing on the Atlantic shore, or the Norwegians migrating into the northern Midwest. We hope that this interdisciplinary exploration of the westward expansion and the role it played in our nation's history will stimulate your students to learn more about their own community and its heritage as a frontier.

The Concept of the Frontier: A Background Study of the Westward Expansion

The westward expansion has been revived as one of the most popular subjects for study and debate in American history. Historians have reexamined the westward movement and the West and have attempted to separate the West of reality from the West of romance and myth. It has not been easy. Our notions of the West have been colored by movies, television, literature, and art. The new scholarship of the West has had to cut through the West of our imagination and lay bare the West of fact, with all of its unpleasantness—racism, failure, lawlessness, and ecological disaster.

As teachers, it is important to expose students to the realities of history, but we must present a balanced view as well. The story of the West and the frontier is a heroic one; it is a great chapter in our nation's history. Nevertheless, we must not let self-congratulation blur the line between truth and fiction. The Student Information Sheet and activities in this unit present a way to introduce students to the concept of the frontier and its role in history.

Westward the Course of Empire Takes Its Way is the title of this mural in the U.S. Capitol, painted by Emmanuel Gottlieb Leutze in 1861.

National Museum of American Art, Smithsonian Institution; bequest of Sara Carr Upton (accession no. 1931.6.1)

Preparation for This Unit: This unit opens itself to class discussion about the concept of frontier and how it has changed over time. It might prove interesting to ask students what images the term "the frontier" brings to mind. Write students' images on the board and see how many of them come from the media.

Student Activities: Worksheet 1 is an opening activity that involves accessing prior knowledge by brainstorming. Students work as a class or in groups brainstorming images of "the West" and then identifying facts behind those images. This activity can act as a springboard to the preparatory discussion outlined above.

Worksheet 2 is a geography-based activity that involves students in the concept that the frontier in America was fluid, that it moved during different time periods. Students locate early settlements and draw routes of exploration on a map of the United States.

Worksheet 3 is a higher-level activity that will involve some individual research as students fill out a chart on other countries' frontiers. It could be done as group work, with each group taking a different country and reporting results of their work to the class. Be sure students draw conclusions from this activity about the importance of the frontier in each of these areas. What did each country want from its frontier? More land for settlement? Exploitation of resources such as timber or minerals? Did any of these frontier areas become as important to their countries as the American West did to the United States?

A good follow-up activity to this entire unit might be to have students construct a display or write a paper on the topic "Frontiers and Pioneers of Today." Are there people today who fit the definition of "pioneer"?

The Concept of the Frontier

What Was the Frontier?

- In 1890, the United States Census Bureau issued a startling report. The frontier had ceased to exist.

- In the 1950's, Walt Disney studios produced a series of TV movies about Davy Crockett. The theme song hailed him as "king of the wild frontier."

- In 1961, President John F. Kennedy called for new domestic policies. He called them "the New Frontier."

- The legendary television series *Star Trek* opened each episode with the words, "Space, the final frontier!"

What exactly was the *frontier** in each of these cases? The concept of the frontier is a complex one with many different meanings. Still, most historians recognize that the frontier in the United States was an important part of our national story.

Frederick Jackson Turner was a well-known Wisconsin-born historian. In 1893, he wrote a paper titled "The Significance of the Frontier in American History." Turner had a specific meaning for the term "frontier." It was the region between land that was settled and "civilized" and land that was unpopulated and primitive. This is a standard dictionary definition for "frontier." The United States, Turner wrote, had always had a frontier area of free, open land. This frontier had kept moving westward. Turner believed the frontier could explain the unique American character.

Since Turner's time, there has been much criticism of his "Frontier Thesis." It had a one-sided approach to explaining American history. Turner's frontier was pushed westward by white settlers. He took no note that the land the *pioneers* wanted had been shaped and lived on for hundreds of years by the American Indians. Also, Turner viewed the frontier as unique to America. Yet many countries—such as Canada, Australia, Russia, and South Africa—have had a frontier region. All had *indigenous* people who lived in the supposed *wilderness*. *They* were often displaced by the newcomers.

Where Was the Frontier?

There have been many frontiers in American history. Settlers moved north from Massachusetts during the late eighteenth century into what is today the state of Maine. There they faced an isolated wilderness area. Survival was possible only by great effort and hard work. The frontier, thus, can be any region where settlement is taking place in an area that is unpopulated and less advanced—by European standards.

The most important frontier in the United States was the one that lay to the west of the Atlantic coast. The line of this frontier—what was known as "the West" at any given time—changed over the years. First, "the West" was the Appalachian Mountains. Then the frontier shifted to an area known today as the Old Northwest. Then it became the area beyond the Rocky Mountains.

(continued)

---

* Italicized words are listed and defined in the glossary at the end of this unit.

The Concept of the Frontier *(continued)*

The Final Frontier

The Great Plains is the area that stretches from the Dakotas to Texas. Interestingly, it was settled later than the Far West of the Pacific coast. Early settlers thought that the Plains was a desert incapable of supporting agriculture. Only after the Far West was settled was it determined that the Plains could, in fact, support farming. *Emigrants* then began to settle this area we now call the Midwest.

Settlement of the West

The westward movement began almost as soon as European colonists landed on the Atlantic shore. Many reasons drove people to emigrate and settle new lands. We'll look at these reasons in detail in Unit 2. The hunger for land was a primary driving force.

Right from the very beginning of our nation, the federal government played an active role in the opening up of land for settlement. As early as 1784, Thomas Jefferson wrote an *ordinance* for the Northwest territories. These were the lands between the Great Lakes and the Ohio River, west of Pennsylvania and east of the Mississippi River. This ordinance provided a plan for the government of the territory. It allowed for the eventual establishment of new states.

More important for the growth of the westward movement was the Northwest Ordinance of 1787. This law provided for the formation of new states, as the earlier ordinance had done. But it also provided for education, constitutional rights, and no slavery in the territory. Legally, the Northwest Ordinance applied

only to the Northwest Territory (later known as the Old Northwest). In fact, it provided a model for settlement of all the lands west to the Pacific. The model was applied as those lands were explored, mapped, and eventually settled.

New Realities About the West

What first comes to mind when we hear the term "the West"? What image do the ideas of the frontier and westward expansion create for us? The answer usually is the movement west across the Great Plains and the Rocky Mountains. No event has become more symbolic, more etched in our imagination, or more portrayed in our popular culture. Countless books, televisions shows, and films have shown white settlers moving across the Plains and mountains. The covered wagon has become a symbol of the pioneering spirit of the American people. Today, though, new attitudes and new scholarship are cutting through the *myth* of the West. These new forces are attempting to present the West's history in a more balanced way.

The "Rugged Individualism" Myth

One myth being challenged is the role of rugged individualism. In American myth, brave and sturdy pioneers accounted for the rapid settlement and development of the West. In reality, larger forces were at work. The federal government, land *speculators*, and large corporations played a very active role. Even today the U.S. government is the largest single landowner in the West. It holds over 50 percent of the western states' land. Moreover, the pioneers who went west for better fortune were not all

(continued)

The Concept of the Frontier *(continued)*

The title of this Currier & Ives lithograph by Frances F. Palmer is *The Rocky Mountains: Emigrants Crossing the Plains.*

successful. Many lost everything in mining ventures and shady land deals. The many ghost towns throughout the West attest to lost hopes and dreams.

The White, Eastern Settlement Myth

Another common myth sees the West being settled from the east by successive waves of whites. In myth, these white settlers came to a virgin land untouched by humans. In fact, the white settlers moving west were only one in a series of migrations. Some American Indian tribes moved from eastern lands into the West long before the colonists arrived from Europe. The Spanish came into the West from Mexico. Asians arrived from across the Pacific. Kanakas came from Hawaii. In the late 1700's, the Russians had a settlement in what is today northern California. Not all of the pioneers who traveled from the east starting in the 1840's

were of European background. African Americans emigrated to the West as well, seeking land and opportunity. Also, the land that the new settlers found was not untouched by humans. It had been shaped by Indian tribes who had lived there for hundreds of years.

The Real Native American Story

The story told about the Native Americans in the West has often not been complete. Tales are told of conflict and deceit. Many movies and paintings show Indians killing innocent white settlers and attacking wagon trains. Yet historians have been hard pressed to find one factual account of Indians attacking a wagon train. Death by Indian attack was not common. *Emigrants* were much more likely to die when the emigrant or a comrade accidentally fired a gun.

(continued)

The Concept of the Frontier (continued)

The real story of Native Americans and the westward movement is complex. It involves the takeover of Indian lands, the reservation system, and the Indian uprisings of the late 19th century. It is important to realize, too, that Native Americans remain part of the West today. In 1890, only 250,000 Indians lived in the West. In 1990, over 2 million did. The culture of the American Indians is as much a part of the heritage of the West as the covered wagon and the pioneer family.

The Environmental Effects

Historians today also emphasize the *environmental* results of the westward expansion. People moving westward looked upon the resources of the West as unlimited. The West's natural wealth was exploited from the very beginning. This often had disastrous results. We'll consider the ecological impact of the westward movement in Unit 5.

The push to the West has great significance for us living in the United States. The story of the West continues to be a symbol of opportunity and hope for a better future. As responsible citizens, it is up to us to understand that no story is complete without a careful look at all viewpoints. No group that played a part should be left out. No consequence should be overlooked. But groups and events have been ignored when they do not fit the ideal or the legend of what happened—rather than the reality. The real story of the westward expansion is exciting enough. No tall tales are necessary.

Glossary of Terms for This Unit

emigrant: A person who is leaving one country to enter another. Early settlers moving to the west were called "emigrants" because often they were leaving the United States to enter a territory not officially part of the U.S. Even though places like Oregon and California were eventually added to the United States, the term *emigrant* remained in use.

environment: The conditions that surround a person or animal; one's surroundings. Usually taken in the natural sense, as in plants or land forms.

frontier: The region of land just beyond or at the edge of a settled or populated area.

indigenous: Referring to people, animals, or plants that are living naturally in a particular area, that are native to it.

myth: A legendary narrative that presents a belief of a group of people or explains a practice or an occurrence in nature (i.e., a rainbow, or changing seasons).

ordinance: A decree or law on a particular subject.

pioneer: A person who originates or helps to open up a new line of thought or activity. Also, a person who is an early settler in a territory.

speculator: A person who engages in a business enterprise where a good profit can be made, but at a considerable risk.

wilderness: An uncultivated and uninhabited region.

Which West Is It?

Directions: The term "the West" brings to mind certain things. What are they? Brainstorm all of the images that come to your mind when you hear this term. Write them in the left-hand column. Working with the whole class or in a smaller group, see if you can challenge your classmates' conceptions about the West. Write the facts in the right-hand column. (Your ideas about the West may be correct!) A sample is provided.

My Own Images	The West in Fact
All cowboys looked like John Wayne.	Many cowboys were African American or Hispanic.

Mapping the First Frontier

North America was a frontier for Europeans during the early period of exploration and colonization. Russia and England each had a presence in what would become the American West. Still, Spanish and French explorers and traders were the most active Europeans. France concentrated on the area along the Mississippi River.

> **Directions:** Use the blank map of North America to locate some settlements and draw routes of exploration. You may need to consult history reference books for some.

SPAIN

Santa Fe—1610
El Paso—1598
Albuquerque—1706
San Antonio—1718
Tucson—1776
Los Angeles—1781
Branciforte (Santa Cruz)—1797

RUSSIA

Fort Ross—1812
Fort Archangel St. Michael—1799

FRANCE

Fort Pontchartrain (Detroit)—1701
Sault Ste. Marie—1668
Natchitoches—1714
New Orleans—1718
Fort de Chartres—1720
Vincennes—1732
Cahokia—1699

ENGLAND

Fort Vancouver—1825
Fort Michilimackinac—c.1763

ROUTES OF EXPLORATION

Marquette & Joliet—1673
La Salle—1679–1682
Coronado—1540–1542
Champlain—1613–1615
De Soto—1539–1543
Vizcaíno—1602–1603
Baranov—c. 1799
de Vaca & Esteban—1528–1536
Bering & Chirikov—1741
Cabot—1497–98
Cabrillo–Ferrer—1542–1543
Onate—1598, 1601, 1604–1605

Mapping Directions: Remember, whenever you create a map you must also include a map key or legend. In the legend are the map's title, symbols and their meanings, and the cartographer's name (in this case, your name). Show the symbols for all the routes of exploration in the key. You may certainly be creative with the symbols you use.

(continued)

Heading West

Mapping the First Frontier *(continued)*

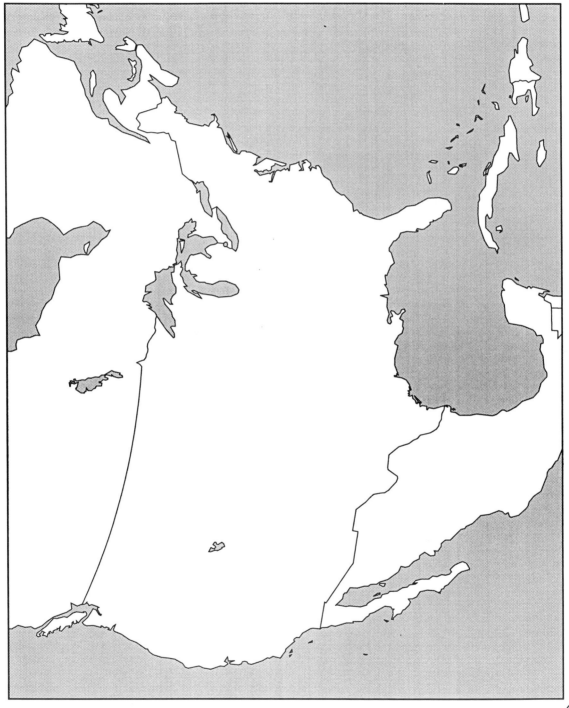

Other Frontiers—An Extra Challenge

Directions: Countries other than the United States have had frontier regions as well. Fill out the following chart on these other frontiers. This may require you to do some research on your own.

COUNTRY	Russia	Australia	Canada	South Africa	Other (your idea?)
Location of Frontier Area					
Role of Government in Settling This Area					
Reason for Settlement					
Geographical Obstacles					
Indigenous Peoples					

Heading West

Reasons for the Move West

Given the hardships experienced by the early pioneers on their trip west, it is important to examine their reasons for undertaking the difficult journey. The objective of this unit is to explore the diverse reasons for westward expansion. The motivations range from a desire for freedom from religious persecution to a quest for riches and adventure. "Land hunger," the yearning for more and better farmland, appears to have been a major reason for the movement to the West, both to the Far West of Oregon and California and, later, to the Great Plains.

Preparation for This Unit: A good preliminary activity might be to initiate a class discussion on reasons people move today. Students may be able to share personal experiences about why their family has moved or why they have stayed put. Have they moved because of job changes? educational opportunities? to be with family? A follow-up activity could be to examine reasons for relocation today compared with the emigrants of the nineteenth century.

Student Activities: Worksheet 1 involves critical thinking in exploring historical causality. Students are given short descriptions of events that occurred during the nineteenth century at the height of the westward movement. Have students work individually, in pairs, or in groups. Assign one or more event descriptions to students. Then tell them to evaluate the impact each event had on the emigration westward, as directed on the activity sheet.

Worksheet 2 is an Extra Challenge activity. Throughout the westward expansion, many settlers were squatters; they occupied a piece of land without legal claim to it. Sometimes, a squatter could legally obtain land by occupying it for a set period of time. The pursuit of land often involved confrontations and misunderstandings over land rights and ownership. Worksheet 2 is a problem-solving simulation based on this issue.

Reasons for the Move West

". . . [I]n the fall of 1849 my father was taken with a heavy case of 'western fever.' He caught the malady from his cousin, who had spent the summer of 1848 in Iowa and had made large investments in prairie lands. He was a good talker and easily persuaded my father that Iowa was the new land of promise, so our farm and all the stock was sold, our household goods were packed in wagons, good-byes were said, and we turned our faces toward the west."[1]

Thus began the story of thousands of settlers who turned their faces westward—in search of what? Since the very first European settlements in America, the colonists had restlessly moved into the frontier areas. Viewing this never-ending movement, one traveler on the National Road in 1817 said, "Old America seems to be breaking up and moving westward. We are seldom out of sight as we travel on this grand track, towards the Ohio, of family groups before and behind us."[2]

Overall Factors

There were many reasons for this urge to head west. Still, we can make a few broad statements about the move:

- Most people who went west went freely. They made the decision to go of their own

free will. The exception to this was some American Indian tribes like the Cherokees.

> The U.S. government forced the Cherokees to leave their southeastern homelands. The army pushed the Cherokees into designated "Indian Territory." The Cherokees called their sad trek to what is today the state of Oklahoma their "Trail of Tears."

- Settlers went west for a better life. Many had moved repeatedly, each time hoping for something better.

- People who moved westward had some money. Moving was an expensive business. Poor people simply did not have the means to make the journey.

- Most people who emigrated were part of a family group. An exception to this was at times when gold and silver were found. Many single men, for example, flocked to California during the Gold Rush.

---

[1]"Memoir of John Culbertson," *American Heritage*, Vol. XVIII, No. 1 (December 1966), p. 84.

[2]Billington, Ray Allen, *Westward Expansion* (New York: Macmillan, 1963), p. 295.

(continued)

12   *Heading West*

Reasons for the Move West *(continued)*

Specific Factors

Land Hunger

Broad statements aside, many diverse reasons caused people to leave the familiar and head out into the relatively unknown lands of the West. Probably the most important urge was the desire for land. Farmers were always looking for better land and more land. They were enticed by stories of fertile soil and huge crop yields. The U.S. government got no money at that time from income tax, so the government made money by selling public lands. It charged as little as $1.25 an acre. Sometimes speculators would buy up land and then try to raise the price. But for the most part, a settler could get land cheaply. Sometimes, land was free. The Homestead Act of 1862 declared that any citizen or intended citizen could claim 160 acres of surveyed government land. People claiming land had to improve it by building a dwelling and growing crops. They also had to stay on the land for five years. If they did this, the land became theirs, free and clear.

Solomon D. Butcher Collection, Nebraska State Historical Society

Photographed outside their new residence in Nebraska are Ephraim Swain Finch and his wife, who started out with very little but eventually prospered.

(continued)

Reasons for the Move West *(continued)*

"Land hunger" also affected people who wanted enough land to divide among their children. Land in the eastern part of the United States was becoming less available and more expensive. So farmers looked to the great expanses of land in the west.

> Land in Europe often could not be divided. Those not lucky enough to inherit land in Europe turned their eyes to the U.S. West. People from Europe often couldn't become landowners in their own countries because of *primogeniture.* In that system, all of a family's land had to be handed down to the oldest son. This left other children out of the family inheritance. Land ownership stayed in the hands of the few. For all settlers, land ownership meant dignity and independence.

Improved Climate

The desire for a better and healthier climate was sometimes a motive for westward expansion. Oregon and California in particular attracted people looking for a pleasant climate. The cold winters of the Northeast and Midwest drove many farmers toward areas with milder seasons. The winter of 1845 was especially frigid. Many emigrants who left for the west in 1846 were responding to that. Health concerns also fueled westward moves. In the Mississippi and Ohio River valleys, malaria was *endemic.* Every year people fell ill with burning fevers and shaking chills. Throughout the Midwest, people suffered from "milk sickness." This was caused by drinking the milk or eating the meat of cows that had grazed on a poisonous plant, the white snakeroot. At the time, the causes of these illnesses were unknown. It seemed that a change in the environment was necessary to avoid them. So many people emigrated to the Far West in search of a healthier place to live.

Religious Freedom

For some settlers, the desire to escape religious persecution led them west. The most famous example is that of the members of the Church of Jesus Christ of Latter-Day Saints, popularly known as the Mormons. They moved a number of times because of persecution. Their final move took them all the way west to what is now Utah.

> Founded in upstate New York by Joseph Smith in 1830, the Mormons had moved several times to escape persecution. They had built the city of Nauvoo in Illinois, which they hoped would be a permanent home. In Nauvoo, the Mormons prospered and their city grew to 15,000. Unfortunately, persecutions began again. In 1844, Smith and his brother were killed by a mob. Nauvoo was in danger of being destroyed. Brigham Young became the new leader. Under him, the Mormons began to look to the Far West for a *zion.* This zion would be a homeland where they would be isolated from the rest of the world and free from persecution. The spot that Young selected was the area beside the Great Salt Lake in what is today the state of Utah. The Mormons carefully planned a mass migration. They left Nauvoo and established a winter camp at Council Bluffs, Iowa. Finally they made their way west to the Salt Lake Basin.

(continued)

Reasons for the Move West *(continued)*

The Mormons moved to escape religious persecution within the United States. Many people, however, came to America to escape persecution in their homelands abroad. They sought freedom and opportunity in the U.S. West. Examples include the Hutterites and Mennonites. These people left Russia to settle in the Great Plains.

The **Hutterites** were German *Anabaptists,* similar to the Amish and Mennonites, who settled the prairies of America in the 1870's. The Hutterites were *pacifists.* This caused them to be driven from their lands many times from the 1600's on. In the 1700's, they were invited to settle in Russia. But in 1874, the Russian government refused to exempt the Hutterites from military service. In response, the Hutterites moved to America. Even in the United States, the Hutterites were not free from all discrimination. Their pacifism caused them many problems during World War I. As a result, many moved to Canada.

Mennonites, like the Hutterites, had moved to Russia. They also immigrated to the U.S. to avoid persecution and settled the Great Plains. They brought with them from Russia a type of red wheat that was highly suited to the Plains. This Mennonite wheat greatly benefited Midwest agriculture.

Better Social Conditions

Some settlers moved for social reasons. Many African Americans found a better life in the West.

- The "Exodusters" were the nearly 20,000 African Americans who moved to Kansas from the South between 1879 and 1880. They were escaping the repression and harsh treatment in the South during Reconstruction. Also, small communities of African Americans were formed throughout the West where jobs were available.

- Clara Brown, a former slave, went west in 1859 as a cook. She was able to start a chain of laundries in Colorado. With her profits, she sponsored other African Americans to move to the West.

- The army in the West was made up of many African-American soldiers. A number of them chose to remain in the West when their term of enlistment was over.

Fortune Seekers

Although many people were drawn to the West to escape harsh conditions elsewhere, some came to get rich quick. These people didn't always intend to settle in the West. They wanted to make their fortune and return to their homes. The so-called Forty-niners of the California Gold Rush were examples of this kind of emigrant. They came West to get rich after gold was discovered in California.

(continued)

Reasons for the Move West *(continued)*

During the Gold Rush, many Chinese immigrated to California. They hoped to make money so they could return to China and live out their lives in comfort with their families. These emigrants were almost always male. Very few brought their families with them, since their goal was not settlement but securing a fortune. A symbol of this motive was the Chinese name for the United States: land of the Golden Mountain.

Manifest Destiny

One of the most debated reasons given for America's expansion was the concept of *Manifest Destiny*. This term was first used in print in 1845. It expressed a belief that it was the absolute destiny of the United States to expand its borders. Also, this expansion was seen as fair and just: The blessings of democracy would be spread over the land mass as well. The idea of Manifest Destiny was used by politicians. It justified the expansion of the United States into territories that had been held by other powers such as Britain and Mexico. Did Manifest Destiny affect an emigrant's decision to take his family into new lands? We don't know. We can't tell how much an individual emigrant thought about the concept.

Economic Cycles

Another possible reason for westward expansion is the impact of economic "panics," or financial *depressions*. Historians debate this issue. For example, the depression of 1837 is often given as a reason for westward migration. People wanted to leave their debt-ridden farms and strike out for a new start. However,

emigrants needed a certain amount of money to leave. Therefore, some historians believe that a period of good economic growth would have stimulated expansion.

Making the Decision

Whatever the reason for moving to the West, the decision-making process was male-dominated. Women had very little say. They had no choice but to abide by the decision of their fathers or husbands. Once the decision was made, women played an important role. They helped prepare the family for the journey. On the trip, they kept the family unit together.

The emigrant had help in making his decision. Many sources of publicity about the new lands to the West were available. Lansford W. Hastings was a rather unscrupulous promoter. He published a book in 1845 called *The Emigrant's Guide to Oregon and California*. This so-called guide made all sorts of outlandish claims about those two regions. In the early years of the westward movement, however, local and familiar sources of information were most trusted. A person's decision about moving was most influenced by the word of his friends or relatives. Letters from local people who had made the journey were much more important than any outside source. This changed after the Civil War. Then, advertising on a national (or sometimes international) scale lured people to the West.

Our restless and mobile society today is still moving. For the most part, our major motivation is still the same today as it was in the 1840's. We move out of a desire for a better life and more opportunity.

(continued)

16

Heading West

Reasons for the Move West *(continued)*

Glossary of Terms for This Unit

Anabaptists: Protestant group originating in Germany in the 1520's who do not believe in infant baptism. Anabaptist groups still in existence today are the Amish, Mennonites, and Hutterites.

depression: A period of low general economic activity with high unemployment.

endemic: Referring to something (usually a disease) that is commonly found in a particular place.

Manifest Destiny: Concept that it was the inevitable destiny of the United States to expand its borders.

pacifist: A person who is opposed to war or violence as a means of settling disputes. Pacifists refuse to perform military service.

primogeniture: System where all inheritance, including land, passes down to the oldest son.

zion: Originally this meant the national homeland of the Jewish people. For other groups such as the Mormons, it came to mean a utopia (a place of ideal perfection), or heaven on earth.

Factors Influencing Migration to the West

Directions: The purpose of this activity is to help you assess those events that caused people to migrate to the Old West. This activity stretches your critical-thinking and problem-solving skills. Read the paragraph(s) assigned to you. Interpret the nature of the event(s) and its (their) relationship to westward migration. Evaluate each event according to how much it would stimulate *significant* migration west. Next, write a paragraph defending your position. If you are working in pairs or groups, you must reach consensus before writing your paragraph.

THE GOLDEN SPIKE. The transcontinental railroad became a reality on May 10, 1869, at Promontory, Utah, when a golden spike was driven and secured the final rail. The nail struck a buried telegraph wire, which announced to the nation that the East and West of the United States were now connected. Building the railroad required thousands of workers. They worked through extreme heat and cold in mountains and deserts.

HOMESTEAD ACT. In 1862, the United States Congress passed an act that allowed people over the age of 21 to receive 160 acres of public land. The person had to be the head of a household, a citizen, or an alien who intended to become a citizen. The person had two ways of getting the land. He or she could pay $1.25 per acre for it. He or she could also get the land free by living on it and improving it for five years.

THE CALIFORNIA GOLD RUSH. In 1848, James Marshall, a carpenter, was busy constructing Sutter's Mill in California. While he was working, he discovered gold. The get-rich-quick news of the discovery spread across the nation. The California gold-seekers of 1849 swiftly became known as Forty-niners.

THE CIVIL WAR. The War Between the States caused tremendous devastation in the South and border states. Farms, plantations, homes, and industry were destroyed. The Southern economy was in shambles. Large numbers of people were without shelter and work.

TEXAS ANNEXATION. U.S. citizens began settling in Texas formally in 1821, when Moses Austin was granted a colony. By the time Texas revolted against the Mexican government, in 1835, more than 20,000 Americans had migrated there. A year later, in 1836, the Republic of Texas was born. Texas became a U.S. state on December 29, 1845. This dramatically increased the size of the United States.

JOSEPH SMITH, JR. Joseph Smith founded the Mormon faith in New York state. Wherever the Mormons settled, difficulties arose that often resulted in violence. Elders of the church were jailed after Smith declared he was a candidate for U.S. president in 1844. Many believed the Mormons violated the rule about separation of church and state. After the Mormons founded the settlement of Nauvoo, Illinois, Smith was murdered while in jail.

(continued)

Factors Influencing Migration to the West *(continued)*

DESERT LAND ACT OF 1877. This legislation promoted irrigation of desert areas in all western states but Colorado. (Irrigation is a watering system for otherwise dry lands.) People could purchase up to 640 acres. They paid 25¢ per acre at the time of purchase. They paid the balance due in three years, after proving they had irrigated their land. The Desert Land Act was well intentioned. However, it failed to keep away land speculators, who were supposed to be unable to purchase this desert land.

THE DIME NOVEL. From the 1860's into the 20th century, the dime novel romanticized the West. Easterners got most of their "knowledge" of the West from the pages of these cheap novels. The hero of the dime novel could do no wrong. He operated in a landscape that was painted as pristine.

PHOTOGRAPHY. Three photographers may lay claim to prominence in western photography: Carleton Watkins, Timothy O'Sullivan, and William Henry Jackson. Each of these men created a visual record of the West's landscape and people. Their photographs gave easterners some real images of the West to add to their imaginary pictures.

THE COMSTOCK LODE. In June 1859, two prospectors named Peter O'Riley and Patrick McLaughlin were nosing around the Washoe Mountains in Nevada. Alongside a spring claimed by Henry Comstock, they discovered a silver vein. The three men entered into partnership and sent ore samples to California. The results confirmed the discovery of the richest mine in history. News spread rapidly throughout the West, and the boom town of Virginia City was born.

RUSSIAN WHEAT. The farmland of the Great Plains depended on plenty of rainfall. The farther west a farmer went, however, the less rain fell annually. Strains of wheat farmed in the U.S. faired poorly under these climatic conditions. Mennonite settlers planted a strain of wheat from Russia that thrived in the Great Plains. In the 1870's and 1880's, most Plains farmers began using this strain.

THE 1870'S. Two events in the 1870's caused financial distress in the nation. The summer of 1871 was unusually dry. Chicago, which depended on wood for its structures, was like kindling. The Great Chicago Fire of 1871 caused about $200 million in damage—that's in 1870's dollars! The economic depression of 1873 shut down many factories, caused widespread unemployment, and closed banks.

THE CHISHOLM TRAIL. Several factors catapulted cattle ranching into a profitable western enterprise during the mid-1800's. Railroads spread. A population explosion in eastern urban areas and the Civil War boosted demand for beef. Cattle drives to railroad hubs became common. One of the most famous of the cattle drive routes was the Chisholm Trail. It was named after Jesse Chisholm, a Texas cattleman. This trail extended from Texas to Abilene, Kansas. Later trails went to Ellsworth, Dodge City, and Hays.

What Should I Do Now?—An Extra Challenge

Directions: Many of the settlers in the frontier were squatters. They settled on the land, farming it and living on it. But they did not pay for the land. They didn't own it. Consider the problem below and propose a solution for the squatter.

I have lived here in this cabin and farmed this land for 42 years. I am now 76 years old. I am all alone except for the farm animals and my old dog.

Yesterday a man came to the door and told me I had to get out of here and find myself a new place to live. He said I have no right to this land because I never bought it.

I said to myself that he must be crazy—I've lived here longer than he has lived!

This morning the sheriff came and told me that I do have to be out of here by sunset tomorrow.

What do I do now?

A Page from the Past

The Amana Colonies

Many groups came to the United States for religious freedom and economic opportunity. Among these were members of the Community of True Inspiration, a church founded in Germany in 1714. Church members believed that God would communicate to followers through an inspired individual. God, they believed, had done this in the days of the biblical prophets. Now God would do it again.

The congregations following this belief began to be persecuted. The Inspirationalists, as they were called, wished to educate their children in their own schools. The Lutheran clergy for Germany opposed this. The Inspirationalists also refused to perform military service. For this, government officials attempted to fine and imprison them. In addition, church members had to pay high taxes and rents. Then a serious drought killed their crops.

To escape all of these problems, church leaders traveled to America in 1842. They had decided to buy land for a new community. They purchased some 5,000 acres near Buffalo, New York. Soon, 800 church members immigrated to the United States. They set up a communal system which remained unchanged for 89 years. All property, except some personal items like clothing, was held in common by all members of the community.

As the community grew in size, it no longer had enough land to support its members. The leaders now looked toward the West. There, land was lower priced and available in large tracts. In 1855, the community moved to Iowa, where they built a village called Amana. The name, taken from the Bible, means "to remain true."

Eventually, the church members built seven villages, covering 26,000 acres. These villages were collectively known as the Amana Colonies. People in the colonies were assigned jobs to perform. There were no paychecks. In return for labor, the community supplied housing, food, education, and medical care to all of its members. Everyone in the community was assigned to eat in a communal kitchen. Each village had several kitchens, with each one serving 30 to 40 people. Girls went to school through the eighth grade. Then their job was to work in the communal kitchens under the direction of an adult woman. Most boys engaged in farm work. There were some other jobs, such as working in the woolen mill, producing textiles for which the Amana Colonies became famous. In fact, the quality of the many items produced by the Colonies was widely known. Their goods were sought after. Amana Refrigeration, a well-known maker of appliances, was once part of the Colonies. Now it is a subsidiary of a private corporation.

In 1932, due to the pressures of the Great Depression, the church members abandoned communalism. People became owners of their own homes and land. They could work for a wage and eat in their own kitchens. The church remained an important part of their lives—and continues so today. In 1965, the Amana Colonies were designated a National Historic Landmark. This means that this site possesses particular significance in our nation's history. Today, the Amana Colonies are an important tourist site in Iowa. Visitors can explore the small villages that still look much the way they did when they were built. Services in German are still held in the village churches. Many of the crafts are made the same way they were in the nineteenth century.

Name _____

Date _____

A Page from the Past

The Exodusters: African Americans Move West

After the Civil War, thousands of African Americans crossed the Mississippi River into the West. The most dramatic part of this movement was the migration of the Exodusters into the state of Kansas. In the spring of 1879, as many as 6,000 blacks fled from the South into Kansas. This was probably the largest mass migration in the years following the Civil War. As many as 20,000 Exodusters may have left the South in 1879 and 1880. The name "Exoduster" referred to the Biblical "exodus" of the Jews from slavery in Egypt. Many African Americans saw their move as part of God's plan.

This migration had two causes: terrorism and high rents. Most blacks struggled against both these problems in the Southern states after the Civil War. Many whites were determined to keep the newly freed slaves from becoming politically active. So they practiced "bulldozing," a campaign of beatings and murder, usually carried out at night. Many white Southerners also felt deprived of their "free" slave labor after the Civil War. In revenge, they charged black tenants extremely high rates to rent farmland. Some blacks felt that they were never going to get out of debt and be able to own land.

North Wind Picture Archives

En Route for Kansas—Fleeing from the Yellow Fever, 1879, is the title of this drawing by Sol Eytinge, done from a sketch by H. J. Lewis.

(continued)

A Page from the Past

The Exodusters:
African Americans Move West (continued)

The election campaign of 1878 was particularly violent in many southern states; this caused "Kansas fever" to take hold. Southern blacks were gripped with the desire to escape poverty and repression by moving to Kansas.

Kansas had special significance for African Americans. Abolitionists—people working to end slavery—had been active there before the Civil War. Benjamin "Pap" Singleton, an elderly ex-slave, believed that it was his mission to bring blacks to Kansas. He worked hard at creating African-American settlements in that state. Some blacks were misled into believing that the federal government would give them free transportation to Kansas—and free land once they got there. Yet many came prepared to buy their own land. The new black settlers bought about 20,000 acres of land.

The trip to Kansas was one of hardship for many families. Southern white landowners were fearful of losing their labor force. So they pressured steamship operators, who refused to transport Exodusters across the Mississippi River. Many families faced disease and starvation while waiting on the river docks. Finally, threatened by lawsuits, the steamboat companies relented. The Exodusters were then able to make their way to St. Louis. From there, they went on to Kansas.

Once in Kansas, the Exodusters did not find immediate prosperity. They remained economically poor. Still, most felt they were better off than they would have been had they remained in the South. By 1886, about 75 percent of the Exodusters owned their homes. Their annual income, though, was on average about 22 percent lower than that of white settlers. Sometimes Exodusters had trouble finding jobs. Then they would move within Kansas or to other states in search of work.

On the whole, Exodusters had a better life in Kansas than in their original Southern states. They were not free from all forms of discrimination, yet they felt more secure. The exodus proved that African Americans cared about their civil rights. They showed that they would not resign themselves to being economic and political victims.

Nicodemus, Kansas, is the only African-American township still in existence from the time of the Exodusters. Nicodemus is the site of the first U.S. post office operated by African Americans. The town was declared a National Historic Landmark in 1974.

Finding a Route

The objective of this unit is to familiarize students with the geography of the United States, particularly the areas west of the Mississippi River. Settlers from the more crowded eastern areas of the United States were astounded by—and often unprepared for—the vast expanses of the West. In the East the climate is wetter, and the mountains, rivers, and other landforms are not nearly as difficult to cross. Emigrants moving west beyond the Great Plains had formidable obstacles to surmount and overcome—steep and rocky mountains, sudden snowstorms, dust storms, deserts, and raging, unpredictable rivers.

Travelers tried many routes west. Although they found hardship, disaster, and death on all the trails, some proved less difficult than others. How were the best routes determined? Students are asked in this unit to put their knowledge of geography to the test to create their own routes to the early frontier of what today is known as the Midwest, and the later routes used to cross the Great Plains and Rocky Mountains safely to the Far West of the Pacific coast. The actual routes used are shown on Worksheet 4, so students can evaluate and compare their trails west with the original routes.

Preparation for This Unit: It would be advantageous if students have some background in geographical terms, such as *plateau*, *desert*, and *canal*. A large physical map of the United States would be helpful to display in the classroom.

Student Activities: The student activities in this unit range from basic to more complex, beginning with Worksheet 1 and progressing to Worksheet 3. The first activity is a basic investigation of landforms in the United States. Students are asked to label a physical map of the United States with the major landforms that might impede or, in some cases, aid migration and settlement. A blank physical map of the United States is included as part of Worksheet 1, but you might wish to enlarge this map to make it easier for students to label. Colored pencils would prove useful as well.

Worksheet 2 involves group work and more critical thinking skills. Students break into groups and study the various landforms found on the way west. They must evaluate the effects these landforms would have on westward expansion, and what would be needed to overcome these obstacles or reap their benefits.

Worksheet 3 enables students to plot their course west from a number of different locations, choosing what they feel would be the best route. They also need to calculate when they would leave each area in order to avoid weather-related problems.

Worksheet 4 shows the actual routes taken by the emigrants. Have students compare their routes with the actual ones.

Finding a Route

Waves of Migration

The history of the United States is, in a very real sense, the story of great migrations.

- The first white migration was that of the Puritans, who fled religious persecution in England. They crossed the Atlantic to settle the northeastern shore of what is today the United States.

- As more immigrants from Europe arrived, and the coast became crowded. People moved farther inland. They settled lands which they believed to be free for the taking, even though Native American tribes lived on these lands.

- The westward movement continued with the passage of the Northwest Ordinance in 1787. This law set up an area known as the Old Northwest as a kind of colony of the United States. It made rules for settling and governing this territory.

The Old Northwest was roughly made up of the land north of the Ohio River. It stretched from Pennsylvania on the east to the Mississippi River on the west. The Great Lakes acted as a border with Canada on the north. This land had rich resources of timber and fertile land. They greatly appealed to the small farmer from the North and South alike. *Emigrants* streamed across the Appalachian Mountains and spread across this new frontier. They traveled by *Conestoga wagon*, flatboat, and/or simple farm wagon. Some of the people who settled the Mississippi Valley were immigrants from Europe. Most, though, were farmers from the older states. This second great migration was most intense from 1810 to 1840.

Paths of Migration

In moving to the Old Northwest, emigrants had several choices. They could use natural highways of travel such as rivers. They could also travel on people-made routes such as *roads* and *canals*.

Emigrants going from Baltimore to Illinois could take the Baltimore Turnpike to Cumberland, Maryland. Then they could continue on the National Road to Vandalia, Illinois. After 1830, many roads were "Macadamized." They were built to the specifications of a Scotsman named John Loudon McAdam. McAdam called for roads to be built of three layers of fine stones, smoothed down with a cast-iron roller. Drainage ditches lined these roads on both sides. In 1825, the Erie Canal was opened. It covered 360 miles from Albany to Buffalo. Soon it became loaded with barges carrying freight and settlers to the West and bringing back raw materials to the East. A canal barge moved at only 1½ miles per hour. Still, it was a cheaper and more efficient way to move bulk goods. In the East, canals soon replaced Conestoga wagons as a method of carrying heavy items. Canals were very useful to move the heavy loads of household goods that westward-bound emigrants would need.

(continued)

Finding a Route *(continued)*

Obstacles to Migration

The *landforms* in the United States east of the Mississippi River did not present difficult obstacles to westward expansion. The rivers were navigable. The mountains were steep but passable. Wide valleys invited travel. Americans who moved west in the first half of the nineteenth century were certainly traveling to a wilderness by East Coast standards. Yet it was a wilderness that had been explored for many years. It was not an environment beyond the settlers' comprehension. With hard labor, they knew that they could begin anew in the wilderness. They would be able to set up communities much like those they had come from.

A striking contrast to this was the area known as the Far West. This included the Rocky Mountains and the land beyond to the Pacific Ocean. The Far West had been explored and charted by government officials, mountain men, and fur trading companies. Yet much of it remained unknown, vast, and ominous. The landforms were very different from the rather mild geography east of the Mississippi River.

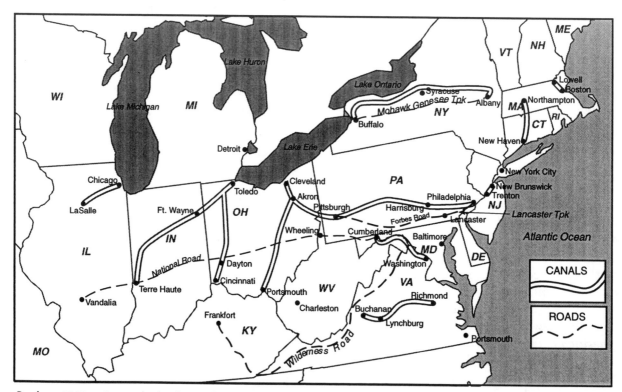

By about 1840, emigrants had a choice of routes to the West, thanks to the development of roads and canals.

(continued)

Finding a Route *(continued)*

- Directly west of the Mississippi was an enormous expanse of grassland. People called it *"The Great American Desert."* (We know it now as the Great Plains.) Because no trees grew there, people thought that this prairie could not support agriculture.

- Beyond the prairie lay the Rocky Mountains, much more rugged and steep than any mountains found east of the Mississippi.

- The Far West also had real deserts, which supported very little life at all and contained no water. In fact, water was scarce throughout much of the far western territory.

The first travelers to the Far West were adventurers who brought little with them. By the early 1840's, families were being lured to Oregon and California. They had to bring with them provisions for the long journey. They also had to haul things to get them started in their new land—plows, hammers, spinning wheels, clothing, furniture.

The true enemies of these emigrants to the Far West were time and geography. Time was important because of the length of the trip. It was 2,000 miles from Independence, Missouri, to the Willamette Valley in the Oregon country. Hauling their heavy loads, most emigrant groups could travel only ten to twenty miles per day. They had to start the trip when the grasses on the prairie first turned green in the spring. This provided needed forage for their animals.

They had to complete the trip before the early snows of autumn fell in the high mountains. The route they chose had to be the one easiest for humans, animals, and wagons to cross.

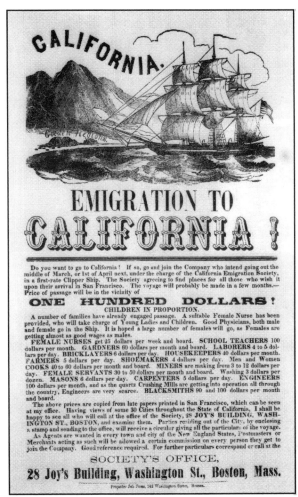

In 1849, the California Emigration Society put out the poster shown in this print: *Emigration to California!*

California Emigration Society; reproduced by permission of The Huntington Library, San Marino, California

(continued)

Finding a Route *(continued)*

The Oregon Trail

The routes that the pioneers used are marked even today with the ruts of their wagons. Up to 500,000 settlers traveled to the Far West. Most took a route known as the Oregon *Trail*.

> This trail took emigrants to both Oregon and California over the Rocky Mountains. After the mountains, most settlers split off from the trail and headed southwest into California.

The Oregon Trail has developed significance of almost mythic size in our history. It has become the symbol for the entire westward movement. Families, not individual adventurers and speculators, migrated west along the Oregon Trail. For this reason, Americans seem to identify more readily with the settlers' journey and their hope for a better life.

Does the "Great Migration" go on even today? The cover of a May 20, 1996, *Newsweek* magazine had as its headlines: "Swimming to Seattle. Everyone Is Moving There. Should You?" In our quest for opportunity, we are still a fluid, mobile society. The routes may be easier, but the spirit of adventure is still there.

> Emigrants were often forced to cross a river or stream. They looked for a shallow place, or **ford**, where they and their animals could wade across. Where it was too deep to cross on foot or horseback, wagons might be floated across. Later, ferries were established to carry people, animals, and goods across.
>
> To get across mountain ranges, emigrants used **passes**—gaps between peaks. Most passes were narrow gorges. But, the South Pass on the Oregon Trail was many miles wide.

> In crossing the Rocky Mountains, pioneers also crossed the **continental divide**. Streams on one side of the divide flow east, and on the other side, west. Pioneers must have been excited to find themselves at last following streams that flowed westward toward the Pacific Ocean.

(continued)

Finding a Route (continued)

Glossary of Terms for This Unit

canal: A channel dug and filled with water to permit transportation by boat, or for irrigation of crops. Most U.S. canals connected natural bodies of water such as lakes and rivers.

Conestoga wagon: Type of wagon developed in the Conestoga Valley of Pennsylvania during the 1770's and first used for the early westward expansion across the Appalachians.

emigrant: A person who is leaving one country to enter another. Early settlers to the West were called "emigrants" because often they were leaving the United States to enter a territory not officially part of the U.S. Even though places like Oregon and California were eventually added to the United States, the term "emigrant" remained in use.

"The Great American Desert": Term that Americans of the first half of the nineteenth century used to describe the Great Plains, which stretched from the Mississippi River to the Rocky Mountains. Because no trees grew there, people thought that the land could not be farmed. Therefore, they reasoned, it was a desert.

landform: A natural feature of the earth's surface such as a mountain range or lake.

road: A route of travel deliberately laid out and constructed.

trail: A route of travel established merely by use.

Getting Prepared

> **Directions:** On the physical map of the United States, label the land-forms and locations listed below. Make a key for your map that contains the title of your map and any symbols you choose to use.

Physical Features

Atlantic Ocean	Great Salt Lake	Appalachian Mountains
Pacific Ocean	Mississippi River	Rocky Mountains
Lake Ontario	Missouri River	Sierra Nevada
Lake Huron	Snake River	Cascade Range
Lake Erie	Ohio River	Blue Mountains
Lake Superior	Platte River	Wasatch Mountains
Lake Michigan		Great Plains

Extra Challenge

Sweetwater River	Humboldt River	Great Basin
Willamette Valley	San Joaquin Valley	

Locations

Independence, Missouri	St. Louis, Missouri	San Francisco, California
Council Bluffs, Iowa	Santa Fe, New Mexico	St. Joseph, Missouri

(continued)

Getting Prepared *(continued)*

Geographic Obstacles to the Migration

Directions: Break into four groups. Each group should take one kind of landform that confronted the pioneers as they moved westward. Describe the landform. How was this landform an obstacle to the emigrants? What did they need to overcome it? Did this landform provide any kind of benefit for the settlers? Share your information with the rest of the class.

Extra Challenge: Choose a specific landform from your labeled physical map (i.e., Sierra Nevada, Snake River) and tell how that landform affected migration.

Plains   **Mountains**

Deserts   **Rivers**

Planning the Way West

Directions: Use the physical map of the United States on which you have labeled the landforms. Draw the route you would take in the situations listed below. Using colored pencils would be helpful for this. At the starting point of your journey, write the month of the year you would begin your trip. Be prepared to defend the reasons for your chosen routes and for your starting date. As a follow-up activity, compare your way west with the actual routes taken by the settlers, shown on Worksheet 4.

1. The year is 1849. You are a young adventurer from Boston, and you wish to reach the California gold fields. How would you travel overland?

2. The year is 1846. Your family wishes to leave their farm in Arkansas and head for the Willamette Valley in the Oregon country. Draw the route you would take.

3. The year is 1840. You wish to travel with 20 bolts of cotton cloth from Lowell, Massachusetts, to Cleveland, Ohio. Plot the cheapest and easiest route.

4. The year is 1832. Your family wishes to leave their farm in Virginia and start anew in southern Illinois. Draw the route you would take.

5. The year is 1835. You are a merchant in St. Louis, Missouri, with several wagonloads of goods you wish to sell in Santa Fe. Draw the route you would take.

Extra Challenge: The year is 1848. You and your family are members of the Church of Jesus Christ of Latter-Day Saints (Mormons) living in Council Bluffs, Iowa. You wish to reach the Great Salt Lake in Utah. You wish to avoid any conflict with non-Mormon emigrants. What route will you travel?

The Routes They Took!

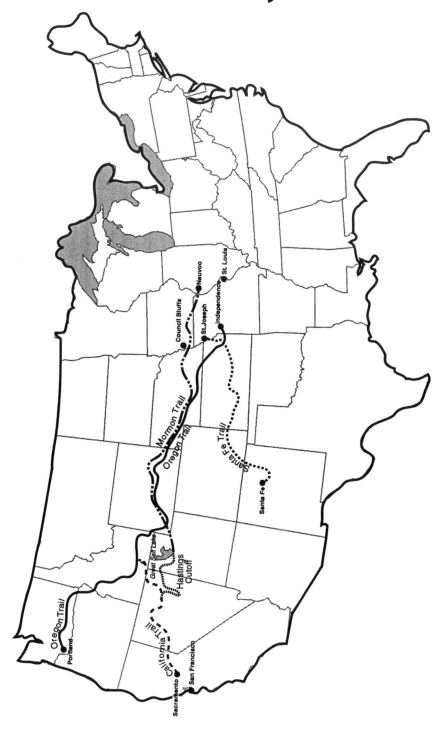

Heading West

Moving West: Wheels, Sails, Hooves, and Rails

Once a family decided to move west, they had to find a practical, affordable means of making that journey. In the early years of the migration, the covered wagon was the vehicle of choice for settlers. Even though the completion of the transcontinental railroad in 1869 brought an inexpensive and fast means of travel to the West, settlers continued to use the covered wagon. It remains a symbol of westward expansion.

The technology of transportation is one that lends itself to interesting discussion and research. Throughout history there has been a quest for a better means of transportation for people and goods. Today, our most important form of transportation is our personal automobile.

Preparation for This Unit: There has always been a dichotomy between the personal, privately owned transport system (horse, covered wagon, auto) and the more public means of conveyance (railroad, steamship, airline). Often the personal transport system leads to crowding and pollution. This was true on the Oregon Trail where, on occasion, wagons backed up for miles and the area around the trail became a wasteland caused by the constant overgrazing of the settlers' stock. With the increasing numbers of people and cars today, can the luxury of private transportation be maintained? How were the problems of transporting large numbers of people solved in the past? These would be good topics for class discussion.

Student Activities: On Worksheet 1, students are asked to examine and analyze the different means of transportation used to move west. They weigh such things as cost, distance traveled per day, and fuel needed in determining advantages and disadvantages of each type of transportation. Worksheet 2 requires some creativity. Students are asked to plan their trip to a frontier of the future, building on the suggested follow-up activity in Unit 1. Worksheet 3 is an Extra Challenge activity dealing with the expansion of the railroads in the West and requiring some individual research.

Moving West

Emigrant families weighed many factors before finally deciding to make the great relocation to the West. How to get there was also a decision that emigrants had to consider carefully. They had to take into account many things:

- How much money did they have for transportation?
- How much and what kind of equipment and supplies did they need to bring?
- Where did they currently live, and where was their final destination?
- How many people would be traveling in their group?
- What travel *technology* was available at that time?

Emigrants chose various forms of transportation. But the greatest symbol of the American westward movement is the covered wagon.

Travel by Wagon

Emigrants into the Old Northwest late in the 1700's had used Conestoga wagons. These huge wagons had carried settlers' families and goods across the Appalachian Mountains. The wagons used to cross the Great Plains to the Far West were different. They were farm wagons with a body or bed like a wooden box four feet wide and ten feet long. The wagon box often had a false bottom about a foot deep. This was divided into storage compartments. More supplies were packed about four feet high on the wagon floor. Wooden bows supported a canvas cloth cover. This was soaked in linseed oil to make it waterproof.

Corel Professional Photos

Oxen pulled covered farm wagons across the Great Plains to the Far West.

The most important part of the wagon was the undercarriage. It had massive axles to support the wheels. A *kingpin* system allowed the smaller front wheels to pivot so the wagon could turn sharp corners over the mountain trails. The wheels were banded with iron "tires." Iron was also used to strengthen certain points on the wagon. The wagon had to meet three other vital standards: It had to be made of well-seasoned wood; it had to be well constructed; it had to be lightweight so the teams of mules or oxen pulling it wouldn't wear out. Despite precautions, wagons broke down and had accidents. In 1850, along one 40-mile stretch of desert, over 2,000 wagons were abandoned. Usually, the oxen pulling them had died of exhaustion.

(continued)

 Heading West

Moving West *(continued)*

> A family of four needed about 1,000 pounds of food for the journey. This included 200 pounds of flour per person, plus 10 pounds of salt, coffee, bacon, and dried fruit.

The trip to Oregon or California took between five and six months. Emigrants had to bring enough food to last for that long. Emigrants also needed personal possessions to help them make a start in their new home. They brought farm implements, cooking utensils, spare wagon parts, even furniture and china. All this was packed tightly in the wagon. Most emigrants walked alongside the loaded wagons to help lighten the load. Even this practice was often not enough of a help. The westward trail was littered with discards. Struggling emigrants would pass by barrels, iron stoves, clothing, piles of rice and beans, and often treasured pieces of furniture.

At the end of the day, travelers formed their wagons into a circle. This was not to ward off an Indian attack. Rather, the circled wagons acted as a corral for the horses, mules, and oxen.

> One common myth about the wagon trains is that they were under constant attack by Indians. This is shown in dramatic paintings and is often a common theme in movies. In reality, most of the settlers who died on route were the victims of accidents or diseases such as *cholera* or *diphtheria*. The Indians were most troublesome to the emigrants by stealing their horses and livestock.

Settlers continued to use covered wagons to move west throughout the 19th century. The wagons provided a relatively inexpensive way to move a large number of possessions a great distance. Over 52,000 people and their wagons traveled the Oregon Trail during the peak migration year of 1852. Even the coming of the transcontinental railroad in 1869 did not end use of the covered wagon.

> Two interesting variations on the covered wagon were the handcart and the windwagon. The Mormons had successfully moved people across the plains and mountains to Salt Lake City starting in 1847. By 1856, very poor Mormon converts, many from the industrial slums of England, wanted to move west. They needed a cheap means of transportation. The answer was *handcarts*. Each one, pulled by one or two people, could carry up to 500 pounds. Five handcart companies, groups of emigrating Mormons, left Iowa City for the Salt Lake Basin. The first three companies reached their destination in nine weeks' time. The last two handcart companies left too late to reach the Rocky Mountains before the winter snows. Rescue teams sent out from Salt Lake City made heroic efforts. Still, over 200 emigrants died from exposure and starvation. Despite this disaster, the Mormons did not abandon their handcart plan until after 1860. Altogether, 3,000 people traveled to the Mormon settlement using handcarts.

(continued)

Moving West (continued)

The constant winds that blew across the Great Plains gave several inventors an idea. They would build a "windwagon," a wagon with sails to propel it across the prairie. *Prototypes* were built, but the problems were hard to solve. How could the wagons be made stable? How could they head in the right direction without having to "tack" back and forth like a sailboat? Windwagons never became practical. The idea ultimately was dropped.

> Even more legendary than the windwagon was the U.S. government's scheme to use camels to carry supplies from Texas to California. In 1855, Secretary of War Jefferson Davis allotted $30,000 for the purchase of 75 *dromedaries*. The camel "express" proved a failure, though. The camels developed sore feet from the rocky surface of the Southwest. Many were turned loose in the desert. Camels terrified horses, cattle, and mules and caused them to stampede. For this reason, many camels were shot by irate ranchers. People claimed to see camels in the western deserts well into the twentieth century.

Travel by Ship

By far, the easiest and fastest way to travel in the early years of the westward migration was by water. Steamboat travel was a very important first stage. Steamboats got the emigrants, their livestock, and their wagons to the "jumping-off points" where they could hit the trail. Steamships could go just so far. No navigable rivers went deep into the interior of the West. No river was more important for the westward expansion than the Missouri, the "frontier highway." The most important route on the river was from St. Louis to the jumping-off points for overland travel such as Independence or St. Joseph. The goods emigrants needed for their trip usually were shipped up the Missouri from St. Louis. Suppliers then sold them (usually at inflated prices!) to the emigrants.

Another way of journeying to the Far West other than land was by seagoing ship. The trip from the East Coast of the United States to California during the Gold Rush of 1849 took four months by sea. The same trip took over six months via the overland route. If adventurers wished to pay more, they could sail to Panama, travel overland across the Isthmus of Panama, and board another ship for California. This was faster than taking the Cape Horn route around the tip of South America. Travel by ship was quicker than by land, but it was expensive. Families with children, animals, and personal possessions usually couldn't afford to go west by ship. Neither could most single people. While some 25,000 miners reached California by one of the sea routes in 1849, an estimated 80,000 went overland.

Travel by Stagecoach and Rail

The stagecoach is another symbol of transportation in the West, nearly as common in our minds as the covered wagon. The stagecoach

(continued)

Moving West *(continued)*

and improved roads to the West cut the time for the overland route to as little as 23 days by 1860. But the $200 fare made this mode of travel too expensive for most settlers. Also, stagecoaches couldn't carry large amounts of freight. Stagecoaches were more important for transportation of mail, money, and paperwork in the West than for large numbers of passengers.

The next dramatic improvement in transportation to the West was the coming of the railroads. In 1869, the driving of the Golden Spike at Promontory Point, Utah, completed the transcontinental railroad. Soon railroads began to be built all over the Great Plains and the Far West. The U.S. government gave railroad companies land grants amounting to millions of acres. In turn, the railroads wanted settlers to

farm these lands. The settlers would then use the railroads to send their crops to market. They would also buy goods shipped from urban centers by rail.

The railroads advertised heavily to draw people to the West, particularly to the previously unsettled Great Plains. The $40 ticket brought rail travel within the reach of all but the poorest members of society. Special "emigrant" trains left from eastern cities. They brought immigrants newly arrived from such places as Russia, Norway, and Germany to the western prairies. The stagecoach might still be used in remote areas where the railroads did not run. But railway travel through the first several decades of the twentieth century was the most popular means of heading to the West.

Kansas State Historical Society, Topeka, Kansas

Crossing a bridge over Canyon Diablo in Arizona Territory was an Atchison, Topeka and Santa Fe Railroad train.

(continued)

Moving West *(continued)*

Glossary of Terms for This Unit

cholera: A disease marked by the loss of body fluids due to vomiting and diarrhea. It is usually caused by contaminated water. In the nineteenth century, it was almost always fatal.

diphtheria: A contagious bacterial disease characterized by a high fever and difficulty in breathing.

dromedary: A one-humped camel used as a beast of burden in North Africa and western Asia.

kingpin: Major bolt by which the front axle and wheels are connected to the rest of the wagon mechanism.

prototype: An original form that serves as a model on which later types can be judged and based.

technology: Applied science; a technical means of achieving a practical purpose.

Choosing How to Go

Directions: Use the chart below to analyze the most common types of transportation people used to move to the West. Evaluate the advantages and disadvantages of each type.

TYPE OF TRANSPORTATION	Fuel Needed	Cost ($)	Distance Traveled per Day	Advantages	Disadvantages
HORSEBACK					
COVERED WAGON					
STEAMBOAT					
STAGECOACH					
RAILROAD					

The Challenge of Modern-Day Frontiers

Directions: Think about possible modern-day frontiers you and your classmates might one day explore. Choose one of those frontiers and imagine you will be pursuing it. What are you going to do?

Spend some time investigating your modern frontier. Then make some decisions about the items below.

Frontier Chosen: _____

Type of Transportation: _____

Clothing: _____

Equipment for the Journey: _____

_____

Equipment for the Frontier: _____

_____

Geography of the Journey: _____

_____

Draw a picture of how you envision your modern-day frontier:

Railroads—An Extra Challenge

Railroads played a significant role in the growth and development of the West during the nineteenth century. Beginning in the eastern states, over 30,000 miles of track had been laid by 1860, reaching into midwestern states. In 1869, the transcontinental railroad was completed, and the entire nation celebrated. Within five years, an additional 30,000 miles of track were laid and opened for transportation of people and goods.

Directions: Use your school or town library, the Internet, or other sources to research railroads in the 1800's. Focus your investigation on four of the best-known lines: the Union Pacific, the Central Pacific, the Baltimore and Ohio, and the Atchison, Topeka and Santa Fe. When you are finished, apply your research to these questions. Write an essay incorporating the answers.

1. Why were the earliest railroad lines built along the eastern seaboard? How did they spread into the Midwest?

2. How did the railroads change the production and sale of manufactured goods?

3. Funding the building of railroads was often "creative." What were some of the ways federal and state governments helped the rail lines? Do you think government involvement was necessary? Describe any alternatives you can think of.

4. In the 1870's, attitudes toward railroads changed. Describe this change, what gave rise to it, and how it affected the railroad business. You should concentrate on steps taken to regulate railroads.

A Page from the Past

Stop Horsing Around! The Real Hero of the Westward Movement Was the Ox

Hollywood movies have given us the image of covered wagons being drawn by high-spirited, quick-moving horses. Not so. The animal of choice to pull the wagons westward was slow-moving and plodding. Most emigrants used oxen as their source of power.

Oxen are neutered male cattle. People have used the ox as a draft animal for hundreds of years. Medieval paintings show peasants in Europe tilling the fields with teams of oxen. Oxford, England, was so named because it was a place where oxen could safely cross the Thames River, literally an "oxen ford." Today, the ox is virtually nonexistent except in "living history" museums like Sturbridge Village in Massachusetts or Lincoln's New Salem in Illinois. But in the eighteenth and nineteenth centuries in America, oxen were a common sight.

In the great migration West, the draft animals had to be trustworthy, strong, and resilient. They had to be able to live off the prairie grasses along the way. Horses were fast, but they needed grain to eat. It was impossible for the emigrants to store and transport large amounts of grain. A few horses did come along on wagon trains. However, they were ridden or led and not worked as hard as the team animals. Later, the trails west were refined into roads. Then horses were used to pull wagons and stagecoaches. The going was no longer so rough, and supplies of grain could be bought along the route.

Many emigrants engaged in heated arguments about using mules to pull wagons. Mules were fast and sturdy. They too could survive on the prairie grass. However, mules were stubborn and cantan-

kerous. Often they did not have the endurance that oxen did. Also, they were expensive. A mule usually cost about $75, while an ox cost $25.

Most emigrant wagons had three yoke of oxen (six oxen altogether). Two yoke was the minimum. Four yoke was the maximum, given the winding mountain trails. One of the saddest stories of the westward move was the fate of these beasts. Many dropped dead of exhaustion along the trail. Many others died from starvation or from drinking bad water. Some were butchered for meat along the trail when food ran low. Pioneer diaries of the trip west contain many notations about dead oxen seen along the way. In one five-day stretch, a settler noted 603 dead oxen. Very few oxen lived to enjoy a quiet rest in the pastures of Oregon or California. Even those who survived the trip often were slaughtered to provide food during the first winter in the new lands.

Peter H. Burnett was an emigrant who went on to become the first governor of California. He wrote, "The ox is a most noble animal, patient, thrifty, durable, gentle, and easily driven, and does not run off. Those who come to this country will be in love with their oxen by the time they reach here." [1] In the story of the move West, the "noble" ox is the unsung hero.

---

[1] Quote from George R. Stewart, "The Prairie Schooner Got Them There," *American Heritage*, Vol. XIII, No. 2 (February 1962), p. 99.

Selling the West: The Lure of Land and Truth in Advertising

"Choice prairie land for sale—low prices."

"Farmers' Paradise!"

"Isn't it time you owned a farm?"

Would-be landowners were bombarded with advertisements attempting to entice them to the West. The railroad companies, as well as state and territorial governments, publicized land sales. They aimed their ad campaigns not only at American citizens but also at Europeans interested in immigrating to the United States.

Land was probably the most important resource possessed by the West. The opening of the Great Plains to farmers in the 1870's brought huge tracts of land within the price range of many who had long dreamed of owning a farm. The area that had been known as "The Great American Desert" was suddenly touted as "The Garden of the West." Very often, the conditions faced by settlers were hardly those one would expect to find in the garden of Eden—terrible temperature extremes, lack of building materials, drought conditions, and plagues of crop-devouring insects. One location in Montana in 1893 had a 164-degree temperature range, from 117 degrees in the summer to 47 degrees below zero in the winter. The pioneers who overcame these obstacles were obviously strong individuals with an incredible will to succeed.

Preparation for This Unit: This unit lends itself well to a discussion of advertising. In the nineteenth century, no governmental agencies oversaw advertisements of various products. Sometimes the claims were quite absurd, but the watchword was "Let the buyer beware!" Should the public be protected from false advertising? Should the farmers who bought land in the Plains have been given their money back if things did not work out as promised?

Another good topic for class discussion would be to look at the climate zones of the West. How do these climate zones compare with those east of the Mississippi? How much of the West appears to be suitable for agriculture without having to rely upon intensive irrigation, which is costly and can have serious ecological consequences?

Student Activities: Worksheet 1 asks students to design their own pamphlet or poster advertising Great Plains land. Students must be sure that (unlike ads one hundred years ago) their advertisements are truthful. The student ads should state risks clearly, rather like the warning labels on medications or the listing of ingredients on other products. Worksheet 2 is a more advanced individual activity that involves statistics and graphing skills. Worksheet 3 is an Extra Challenge activity using critical analysis. Students are asked to examine the chart in Worksheet 2 and the graphs they drew from it and draw some conclusions. This activity includes opportunities for further research.

Selling the West:
The Lure of Land and Truth in Advertising

From the earliest beginnings of immigration to America, the new country was praised, advertised, and often over-sold as a "promised land." In no case was this more true than in the "selling" of the West. Enticing pamphlets, newspaper accounts, letters, posters, and stories were produced. They lured people to move westward, to land available at little or no cost.

Early Promotions

Often the federal or state governments encouraged exploration and emigration. Authorities felt that if settlers moved in to populate an area, the region grew in significance. Settling an area also gave the United States a greater claim to the land. In the late eighteenth and early nineteenth centuries, for example, the government encouraged settlers to move across the Appalachian Mountains into the Ohio and Mississippi valleys and the Old Northwest. Settlers were lured by the promise of available farmland as well as good hunting and fishing.

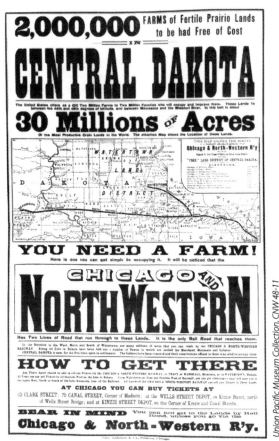

The Chicago & North-Western Railway advertised farms in this *Central Dakota* poster.

Lansford W. Hastings was an early settler of California when it was still controlled by Mexico. Some historians feel that Hastings wanted to rule California as a private republic. To do so, he needed Americans to settle there. Hastings published a guidebook, titled *The Emigrants' Guide to Oregon and California*. The book particularly praised California as the Garden of Eden. According to Hastings, in California oats grew eight feet tall. You needed to kindle a fire only to cook, never to keep warm. The weather was healthful, a perpetual spring. This was just what farmers who had suffered through freezing Midwest winters wanted to hear. Hastings's book was an instant best-seller.

(continued)

Selling the West:
The Lure of Land and Truth in Advertising *(continued)*

Not all territories were opened by governmental authority as was the Old Northwest. Private land *speculators* played a role in picking a likely location for settlement. Then they would publicize its virtues, often distorting and overstating them.

Other publicists wrote pamphlets and letters to the newspapers. They traveled from town to town giving speeches about the healthful, productive conditions in the Far West. One young boy remembered a speaker telling that in Oregon the pigs ran around already cooked. The animals had forks and knives sticking out of them, so you could cut off a slice when you felt hungry! Not all of the tales were as tall as this. Still, to people who were looking for a better place, the stories were tantalizing. Friends and relatives who had emigrated sent positive letters back home. They wrote happily about the lack of disease, the fertility of the land, and the mildness of the climate in the Far West.

Settling the Great Plains

After the Civil War, states, territories, and railroads used mass advertising to coax settlers to western lands. Much of the land that was for sale was in the Great Plains. This land had once been known as "The Great American Desert." To sell land and attract settlers, railroads and states now described the Plains as "The Garden of the West." Ads used the slogan "Rain follows the plow." Supposedly, plowing up land for farming caused rainfall!

Each western railroad and state government had a land department and an agency to advertise for settlers. Possible immigrants from Europe were also targets of ad campaigns. In 1882, the Northern Pacific Railroad printed over 600,000 pamphlets in Swedish, Dutch, Danish, and Norwegian as well as English. Transatlantic steamship companies often got involved in advertising western lands as a way to boost their ticket sales. The railroads and states could sell settlers six times the land they could gain under the Homestead Act. The land was not free, but the terms were attractive. Settlers were offered low prices per acre, credit terms, and special passenger rates. Often special assistance, such as maps or information about agricultural techniques, sweetened the deal.

One prominent immigrant group was the Norwegians, who settled on the grasslands of western Minnesota and the Dakotas. Norway lost more of its population to immigration than any other European country with the exception of Ireland. The advertisements for free or cheap land were important enticements for Norwegian farmers. Land ownership for them or their children in Norway was often not a hope because of strict laws of *primogeniture*. Norwegians already in America wrote guidebooks for immigrants. They set up immigration networks to get information back to Norway about the availability of land. Often Norwegian settlers loaned money to relatives back home so they could make the journey. Successful Norwegian farmers in the United States paid the passage for workers in exchange for labor on their farms.

(continued)

Selling the West:
The Lure of Land and Truth in Advertising *(continued)*

Railroads also sponsored free trips into western lands for newspaper reporters to view the railroad lands that were for sale. The railroad often lavishly entertained these reporters, so they were unlikely to write anything negative when they got home. People thinking about buying land could also travel to see acreage before they made the move. Often the price of their ticket was deducted if they did buy land. Many though, did not visit first, particularly if they were immigrants from overseas. They depended on information in the railroad and state advertisements. They also learned about the land from letters from relatives or friends who had gone on ahead. But sometimes even personal letters were not to be trusted. Immigrants very often tried to justify their decision to leave home by exaggerating their successes and downplaying any problems.

Approximately 14 million Europeans immigrated to the United States in the 1870's and 1880's. Although some settled in urban areas, many came to the Great Plains for land.

What the Ads Didn't Mention

As thousands of people moved to the so-called Garden of the West, what exactly did they find there? Very often conditions were not what they expected. For one thing, the Plains had no forests for timber. Settlers were forced to live in dugouts or sod houses until they could earn enough to buy lumber brought in by railroad. Sod houses, or "soddies," were constructed by cutting the *sod* of a field into one-foot by two-foot blocks. These blocks were put together to form a house. Soddies provided

Solomon D. Butcher Collection, Nebraska State Historical Society

Nebraska farmer Ephraim Swain Finch found his fields besieged by grasshoppers.

(continued)

Selling the West:
The Lure of Land and Truth in Advertising *(continued)*

good insulation from the extremes of temperature on the Plains. However, they were dirty, and water ran through the roof. Snakes and other animals often crawled out from the walls. Since there was no wood for fuel either, settlers used "buffalo chips" (dried bison dung) or even prairie grass for heat and to cook.

The climate of the Plains was *dry continental*, which means sub-zero winters and blazing hot, dry summers. In winter, blizzards could kill any creature caught out in them. For protection, farm animals were often brought into soddies. In the spring, flash floods could sweep away houses, barns, and livestock. Summer and fall brought the danger of prairie fires. These killers could be started by a lightning strike or even the discharge of a gun. Prairie fires could burn for as long as six weeks and could totally wipe out a family's crops and farm tools. Settlers had to learn to set "back fires," which prevented the spread of prairie fires.

Probably the biggest hazard on the Great Plains was drought. The 1880's, when many settlers were moving onto the Plains to farm, had a period of rainfall. By the 1890's, the Plains had entered a dry period. Many settlers were forced to give up their farms and move east. Finding water for Plains farming was essential. Under the Great Plains are a series of

aquifers. However, the depth at which water can be found varies from a few feet to several hundred feet. Farmers had to dig a well and then use a windmill to pump the water to the surface. This was often a very expensive operation. After some time, farmers learned new farming techniques that helped them adapt to the dry conditions. But even today, drought in certain areas of the Plains is a serious problem.

Another disaster never mentioned by the publicists for the Plains were the plagues of grasshoppers that could occur. In 1874, grasshoppers were so numerous on the northern prairies that their swarms looked like storm clouds. Grasshoppers would land and eat all the crops in a matter of minutes. They even stopped trains. When they landed on the tracks, the trains ran over them. Their crushed bodies were so numerous that the tracks became slippery and the trains couldn't move.

The remarkable thing about the selling of the West is not that so many people came to settle, but that so many stayed to tough it out. Their experiences became the subject of many books and stories. They are a symbol of the resilience of the pioneers who risked much to make The Great American Desert the heartland of American agriculture.

Glossary of Terms for This Unit

aquifer: A layer of rock, sand, or gravel that holds water.

dry continental: A climate of extremes with very cold winters and hot, dry summers.

primogeniture: System in which all inheritance, including land, is passed down to the oldest son.

sod: The surface layer of grass and soil filled with roots.

speculator: A person who engages in a business enterprise where a good profit can be made, but at a considerable risk.

Come to the West!

Directions: You are to design a *truthful* pamphlet or poster advertising Great Plains lands for settlement. Be certain to include a "warning label" stating the risks involved in settling in this western area. Be creative in your drawing and wording. How can you convince people to come, given the risks involved?

Where Did the People Come From?

Introduction: By 1900, the white population in many of the Great Plains states owed much to European immigration. Four of these states—North Dakota, South Dakota, Nebraska and Kansas—had a significant immigrant population. Indeed, over 70 percent of North Dakota's population came from European roots. The following statistics indicate the significance of European immigration in four Great Plains states.

COUNTRY OF ORIGIN	North Dakota	South Dakota	Nebraska	Kansas
Austria	2,014	1,692	8,085	6,329
Bohemia	3,654	6,361	38,471	7,788
Denmark	7,139	10,450	26,418	6,687
England	7,710	12,402	33,586	45,633
France	582	835	2,897	5,813
Germany	32,393	55,860	191,928	131,563
Ireland	11,552	16,017	45,535	48,525
Italy	731	566	1,278	1,543
Norway	71,998	51,191	7,228	3,726
Poland	2,112	1,146	7,328	1,478
Russia	23,909	25,689	14,537	25,048
Scotland	5,664	3,943	9,818	14,186
Sweden	14,598	17,163	54,301	35,219
Total including other European immigrants	277,690	231,362	478,622	379,961
Total state population	319,146	401,570	1,066,300	1,470,495

(continued)

Where Did the People Come From? *(continued)*

Directions: Using the data on page 51, complete the following activities.

1. On a piece of graph paper, construct a line and/or bar graph of the information for each state. Label the countries of origin on the horizontal axis and the population on the vertical axis.

2. Calculate the percentage of immigrant population for each state. Then, graph your results using a line and/or bar graph. Label the states on the horizontal axis and the population percentages on the vertical axis.

Why Did the People Settle Here?
An Extra Challenge

Directions: Your graph and statistical chart from the previous activity indicate that Germany, Ireland, Norway, Russia, and Sweden supplied the most immigrants and their descendants to the four states. Answer the questions below using the chart and other sources of information. You may need to do a little research on your own to find the information required to answer some of the questions.

1. Which was the country of origin for the greatest number of immigrants to North Dakota? South Dakota? Nebraska? Kansas?

2. By far, most of the Norwegians settled in the Dakotas. Why do you think this was so?

3. Most of the Irish immigrants settled in Nebraska and Kansas. Why would they do this?

4. What conditions in these five countries led to the emigration of their people?

5. Conversely, what attracted immigrants to these particular states?

6. Choose one of the following roles and imagine you are that person immigrating to the United States. Describe the reasons why you are migrating. Tell the state you are immigrating to and why. In story/journal form, tell about your journey and the decisions you must make. What preparations must you make for your trip? What skills do you have? What will you bring with you? What do you know about the land you are going to live on? What are your expectations?

Roles:

Irish potato farmer   Swedish logger

Norwegian fisherman   German shoemaker

Russian wheat farmer

A Page from the Past

Levi Strauss—A Success Story of the West

For many people, the road west was not paved with riches. They returned home worse off than they had been. For one early immigrant, though, the Far West proved to be a true land of opportunity. After his parents died in 1848, Levi Strauss emigrated from Bavaria to New York City. There, he joined his older brothers, Jonas and Louis. Levi was only 17 years old and knew no English. He took up peddling dry goods (cloth, thread, pins, etc.), which was a fairly common occupation for Jewish immigrants. After six years, Strauss had earned enough money to book passage to San Francisco, California, where his sister and her husband lived.

The trip cost Strauss $400 and took three months. But he soon made up for the cost by quickly selling the merchandise he had brought with him. Other merchants rowed out to his anchored ship to buy up everything he had brought with him. Strauss saw that San Francisco, with its "Gold Rush Fever" and rapidly expanding population, needed goods.

Strauss wasted no time. With his brother-in-law as a business partner, he set up a little dry goods shop in what amounted to a shack. Strauss began to rush aboard incoming ships and buy whatever they had to offer. He then peddled goods from the back of a wagon in the mining camp towns and settlements. The variety, price, and high quality of his goods gained him many customers.

Many businesses failed after the early years of the Gold Rush. Strauss, though, was able to expand. He built a store on a main street in San Francisco that sold $3 million worth of goods. A turning point came when a Jewish tailor in the Nevada territory wrote to Strauss to tell him about a kind of work pants he had devised. The pants were made of cotton duck fabric and were reinforced by copper rivets. The tailor, Jacob Davis, signed a joint patent with Levi Strauss in 1873. Davis then moved to San Francisco to oversee the production of these pants, originally labeled "waist high overalls."

The Strauss and Davis pants and other clothing products were designed for working people. They were an immediate success among farmers, miners, mechanics, and other workers. The pants were usually made from a heavy-weight cotton material known as "jean." Each pair came with a guarantee promising a new pair free if they ripped. The company trademark became a picture of two horses trying to tear a pair of Strauss pants apart.

Part of the legend of Levi Strauss says that when he was first in San Francisco, he was selling canvas tents for miners. A customer approached and told him that the miners didn't need tents. Instead, they needed a good strong pair of work pants. Thus "Levi's" were born. This is a good story, but it isn't true. The real story of Levi Strauss is remarkable enough without made-up legend added to it. A young Jewish peddler made his way west and used his skills to found a multi-million-dollar company. This is a genuine success story of the westward expansion.

The Environmental Impact of the Migration Westward

One of the most visible topics of recent years in newspapers, magazines, books, and broadcast media has been the environment. The misuse and depletion of the resources of the West in particular have been debated and written about extensively. This unit only scratches the surface of the topic, but it can provide a jumping-off point for further class study and discussion.

Preparation for This Unit: A worthwhile class discussion might be to look at local environmental issues. What resources and ecosystems are threatened in the school community? People need jobs in order to live. What happens when environmental issues threaten those jobs, as in the case in which the timber industry has been restricted from working in the habitat of the spotted owl in the Pacific Northwest? Issues like these lend themselves to role-play and simulation, with some students taking the side of the environmental activists and other students role-playing the parts of people whose livelihoods are threatened or harmed by laws designed to protect the environment.

Student Activities: Worksheet 1 is a research activity to familiarize students with the wildlife of the prairie ecosystem and how this ecosystem has been changed by human actions. Worksheet 2 is an exploratory activity that has students look at the plant life of the prairie and determine how many of our common garden plants have their origins in the prairie habitat. Worksheet 3 is an Extra Challenge activity that provides data for students about comparative water use in the East and West. Students' challenge is to display that data in a chart, graph, or diagram. All three of these activities are suitable for individual or group work.

The Environmental Impact of the Migration Westward

The first white American settlers arriving in California were amazed at what they saw. Masses of blue, lavender, and yellow wild hyacinths covered the hillsides. The Indians used the hyacinth bulbs as food. Every year young women dug the bulbs up, split them, and replanted some. With this treatment, the bulbs thrived. The hillsides burst with brilliant bloom year after year.

Within 50 years after the arrival of the Forty-niners for the Gold Rush, the Indian women had been driven off, killed by disease, or murdered. Without their careful management, the wild hyacinths disappeared as well.

This story is one of some significance in the history of the West. For hundreds of years the Native Americans had used the western environment. Their use never destroyed the landscape or wiped out entire species. The massive movement of white settlers into the West changed the delicate balance of nature.

The settlers came from areas in the East, or from Europe, where land was scarce and people were many. They moved into an area that seemed to have endless land and unlimited resources, all there for the taking. The settlers had no sense of the need to conserve or preserve resources. The abundance of the West seemed unending. If resources were used up in one area, there was always another area to exploit. Settlers could move on to another mountain, another river, another tract of land.

The topic of the environmental impact of the westward expansion is one of great depth and much information. To give you an introduction to this subject, we'll look at three areas:

mining in the West, the cultivation of the prairie, and water use.

> Many more topics are available for you to research on your own. Examples are the clear-cutting of timber, river diversion, hydroelectric projects, and nuclear testing in the Southwest.

A key fact is that in the nineteenth and early twentieth centuries, the economy of the West was "extractive." Resources were discovered in nature, extracted or exploited, and then shipped somewhere else to be processed and/or used. Lumbering, fishing, farming, and mining were examples of this kind of activity in the West.

Mining

One of the first resources that drew people to the West in great numbers was minerals, particularly gold and silver. The early mining, like that practiced by the Forty-niners, was usually done by individuals. Some miners panned for gold in streams. Other practiced placer mining. This involved diverting stream water into a trough and sifting for gold nuggets or flakes. When the initial rush was over, the surface riches were gone. Mining then became an industry. Large corporations practiced hydraulic, below-surface, or strip mining.

(continued)

The Environmental Impact
of the Migration Westward *(continued)*

Hydraulic mining was particularly destructive. Miners would use water cannons to blast hillsides and wash away the surface gravel to expose any gold deposits. Entire mountains would be washed into rivers, clogging them with debris. The water became unfit to drink. It flooded farmlands and settlements. Hydraulic mining destroyed acres of valuable farmland and forced a legal battle in California between farmers and miners. This eventually resulted a court decision outlawing hydraulic mining.

Underground mining was also environmentally destructive. The mines of the Comstock Lode in Nevada required an estimated 600 million feet of timber as supports within the tunnels. An additional 2 million cords of wood fueled the nearby mining towns. Entire forests were denuded to support mining. The mine *smelters* severely polluted the previously clean western air. In Butte, Montana, the sulfurous smoke from the smelters was so bad that the people could hardly find their way along the streets even during daylight hours.

Strip-mining scarred the landscape in many western states. In this type of mining, an entire hillside was literally stripped away by power shovels to expose the ores. When the ore ran out, the hillside was left stripped and barren.

In most cases when a mine, a mountain, or a mining town lost its usefulness, it was simply abandoned. Mine operators gave no thought to *reclamation.* Only recently have environmental groups been working to undo the damage and blighted landscapes left by widespread mining in the West.

Cultivation of the Prairie

A second major activity had a great environmental impact on the western landscape: the settlement and cultivation of the Great Plains. This resulted in the destruction of the prairie *ecosystem.* At first, settlers only passed through the Great Plains on their way to Oregon, California, or Utah. They were astounded by the size of the prairie. The grassland area covered one ninth of the North American continent.

The prairie grasses were labeled tallgrass and shortgrass. Their roots went as deep as 11 feet into the soil. This preserved moisture and added nutrients to the soil. The prairie abounded with animal life. It was home to millions of buffalo, pronghorn antelope, elk, deer, prairie dogs, wolves, ferrets, and foxes. Over half of the wild ducks on the continent were (and still are) hatched in the pothole region of the prairie, an area of wetlands in North Dakota.

(continued)

The Environmental Impact
of the Migration Westward *(continued)*

Even the emigrants just passing through the prairie changed this environment. The emigrants' stock animals overgrazed areas of the plain, causing *erosion*. Whites hunted down buffalo—first for food, but later simply for sport. The buffalo population went from an estimated 30 million in 1830 to just 20 animals left in Yellowstone Park by 1897. Other animal species were also hunted with no view toward conservation.

In the 1870's, settlers began to cultivate the prairies of the Great Plains. John Deere had recently invented the self-scouring, steel-blade plow. This made it possible to cut through the prairie sod. By World War I, there was a world-wide demand for wheat. American farmers plowed and planted even more of the Plains, stripping the land of its native grasses. The "Great Plow-up," as it was called, was the recipe for disaster. It struck in the 1930's when a drought hit the Great Plains. The plowed ground lay bare to the wind, and the soil simply blew away. During this Dust Bowl, thousands of people moved from the Plains to California, or even back East. Even today, the Plains states are losing population. Nebraska has over 5,000 deserted farmhouses.

What could have prevented this disaster? In their quest to get ahead, farmers plowed the land bare. When it didn't prove as productive as they wished, they moved on. Large tracts of land were left unplanted. Cattle were allowed to overgraze certain areas. The destruction of the buffalo also caused the prairie to dry out. Buffalo have very sharp hooves, which puncture the sod. This adds air to the sod and allows it to absorb water. Today the use of improved dry farming techniques and the use of the High Plains *aquifer* for irrigation has made the Plains productive once more. Still, the specter of drought is always in farmers' minds. There are also many initiatives to reclaim parts of the Plains as a prairie preserve. Today 10,000 acres of prairie are protected. Even the buffalo has made an astounding comeback to a population of over 200,000.

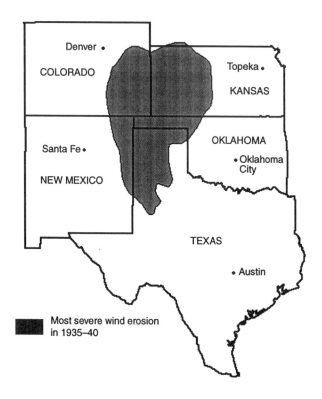

Most severe wind erosion in 1935–40

(continued)

Heading West

The Environmental Impact
of the Migration Westward *(continued)*

Water Use

Many historians of the western environment believe that the single most important resource in the West is water. The 100th meridian separates America into a dry zone to the west and a wet zone to the east. Much of western land is in that dry zone. Adequate supplies of water have been a key to success in the West. They have made settlement of states like California possible.

Much of California is desert. Without a source of water, heavily populated cities like Los Angeles could not exist. The people of Los Angeles use trillions of gallons of water annually. This is much more water than the city and its surrounding land can provide. In 1913, the

Los Angeles *aqueduct* was constructed. It brought water 233 miles from the Owens Valley east of the Sierra Nevada. The valley's potential for agricultural development was destroyed to provide the city with enough water to meet its growing population.

As the population of Los Angeles has continued to grow, so have its water needs. Water has even been brought to the city by aqueduct from the Colorado River, 242 miles away. So much of the river water is diverted for agricultural and urban use that the Colorado is a trickle by the time it enters Mexico. Environmentalists are concerned at the increasing use of western water. They are using conservation efforts for this limited resource.

Kansas Pacific Railway, 1870. DeGolyer Library, Southern Methodist University, Dallas, Texas (collection no. Ag82.86.60)

The Kansas Pacific Railway used buffalo heads for advertising purposes, as shown in this photo by Robert Benecke.

(continued)

The Environmental Impact
of the Migration Westward *(continued)*

In 1941, Los Angeles began drawing water from the streams feeding into Mono Lake. This caused the level of the lake to fall 41 feet. Mono Lake has a unique wildlife ecosystem. A type of brine shrimp lives there that provides food for migratory birds. Evaporation and the loss of incoming water have increased the salinity of the lake and threatened its ecosystem.

Environmental groups took the city of Los Angeles to court. In 1991, a landmark court ruling barred the city from diverting Mono Lake's water until the lake level rises high enough to maintain the wildlife habitat. The city is challenging the court decision.

In the Great Plains, the depletion of the High Plains aquifer has been a matter of some concern. Also known as the Ogallalah, the aquifer was formed over millions of years. Rain eroded the Rocky Mountains and washed gravel and sand onto the Plains. These sediments soaked up rain and snowmelt. The result was a huge underground sponge holding enough water to fill Lake Huron. The discovery of how to tap this resource transformed the Dust Bowl areas of the 1930's into productive farmland. Now, however, the Ogallalah's water is being pumped in some areas faster than rain can replace it each year. Efforts at better management of the aquifer resources have slowed the rate of water level decline somewhat. But water conservation is still a great concern on the Plains.

The West is a land of balance between wilderness and civilization, plenty and scarcity. We also need to be balanced in our view of the people who headed West to make use of its land. According to historian Patricia Nelson Limerick, "[I]n the late twentieth century, when it has become commonplace to hear denunciation of the despoiling of western resources, the rape of the land, the ecological and moral horror that was western expansion, it is important . . . to recall that many of these 'despoilers' wanted primarily to find a job and make a living."[1] How much can they be blamed for failing to realize how much damage they were doing?

[1] Patricia Nelson Limerick, *The Legacy of Conquest: The Unbroken Past of the American West.* (New York: W.W. Norton, 1987), p. 133.

Glossary of Terms for This Unit

aqueduct: A channel or pipe designed to carry water from a remote source.

aquifer: A layer of rock or gravel that holds water.

ecosystem: Organisms and their environment considered as a unit.

erosion: The natural process by which material is removed from the earth's surface, particularly by wind or water.

hydraulic: Moved or operated by a fluid, especially water, under pressure.

reclamation: Restoring something to productivity and usefulness.

smelter: A place where ores are melted or fused to separate their metallic components.

What Has Happened to Them?

Directions: One very interesting study of the western environment is to look at the wildlife of the West, particularly some prairie species that have been threatened. What can you find out about these unique animals of the American West?

ANIMAL	HABITAT	THREAT TO ITS EXISTENCE	PRESENT STATUS
Black-footed ferret			
Prairie dog			
Audubon bighorn			
Elk			
Sandhill crane			
Passenger pigeon			

Hoe! Hoe! Hoe!
Garden Plants from the Prairie

Directions: Gardening is a popular pastime today. Yet very few people realize that many of our most popular garden flowers originally grew wild on the prairie. Below is a list of common flowers found on the American prairie. The list gives both the common name and the scientific name of each flower. Use a garden book and/or a trip to a local nursery center to answer this question: **How many of these flowers do we use today in our gardens?** Circle the names of those you find.

shooting star *(Dodecatheon meadia)*

prairie coreopsis *(Coreopsis palmata)*

downy phlox *(Phlox pilosa)*

wild bergamot *(Monarda fistulosa)*

black-eyed Susan *(Rudbeckia hirta)*

coneflower *(Echinacea)*

butterfly weed *(Asclepias tuberosa)*

New England aster *(Aster novae-angliae)*

showy goldenrod *(Solidago speciosa)*

blazing star *(Liatris spicata)*

sunflower *(Helianthus mollis)*

downy gentium *(Gentium puberulenta)*

compass plant *(Silphium laciniatum)*

pasqueflower *(Anemone patens)*

prairie smoke *(Geum triflorum)*

prairie violet *(Viola pedatifida)*

Water Resources—An Extra Challenge

Directions: The figures below give the amount, in millions of gallons, of water used in the East and the West of the United States per day for various purposes. Your challenge is to construct a graph, chart, or diagram to compare these usages.

EAST	WEST
170,063 million gallons per day	165,346 million gallons per day
—withdrawn per day from resources—	
(millions of gallons)	(millions of gallons)
10,953 irrigated agriculture	145,823 irrigated agriculture
20,529 domestic and commercial use	7,634 domestic and commercial use
46,282 manufacturing	4,554 manufacturing
86,572 energy producing	2,308 energy producing
4,750 mineral producing	2,243 mineral producing
977 other uses	2,784 other uses
88% used and returned	48% used and returned
12% not returned	52% not returned

A Page from the Past

The Dust Bowl:
When the Land Seemed to Blow Away!

On Sunday, April 14, 1935, an enormous black cloud appeared from the north and a storm rolled down on part of Oklahoma. This was no ordinary storm. Unfortunately for farmers, it contained no rain at all. This was a dust storm, the magnitude of which had never been seen before. Car ignitions shorted out. People were lost a few feet from their homes, and the day became as dark as night. Later, that day was referred to as Black Sunday. It was only one terrible event in a terrible decade on the southern portion of the Great Plains that came to be known as the Dust Bowl.

The Dust Bowl was not really shaped like a bowl. It was an area of high, level land that included parts of Oklahoma, New Mexico, Colorado, Kansas, Nebraska, and Texas. The outbreak of World War I in 1914 cut off supplies of Russian wheat to the European market. Europeans came to rely on imports of wheat from the United States. From 1914 to 1919, farmers in the southern Plains states plowed up 11 million acres of native grasslands to expand their wheat production. Fabulous fortunes could be made. Ida Watkins of Kansas became known as the Wheat Queen when she made a $76,000 profit on her 2,000 acres of wheat. Some people became "suitcase" farmers. They drove from place to place with their farm equipment, planted wheat, moved on, and planted more wheat (perhaps in a different state). They returned to harvest their crops months later.

Some people made fortunes from this "Great Plow-Up." Others were small-time farmers who just wanted to make enough money to pay for their land and support their families. It seemed as if the good times were going to last forever. So most people didn't save the money they were earning. Instead, they used it to buy more land to plant more wheat. In 1931, Plains farmers produced so much wheat that the grain elevators couldn't hold it all.

The good times did not last. The stock market crash of 1929 began to affect agriculture. The price of wheat fell from one dollar a bushel to 25 cents. The overproduction of wheat caused the price to fall more. The final blow came when the rain stopped falling. Almost the entire decade of the 1930's was a time of drought. Twenty states set records for dryness during those years.

The low prices for wheat and the drought caused many of the "suitcase" farmers to leave the land. Their plowed fields lay abandoned. With all the dry land exposed to the winds, the dust storms began. People found dust everywhere. It was in their bathtubs, in food containers, on furniture and dishes, in people's hair and ears. People hung wet blankets over the windows at night to try to stop the fine dust from blowing into their houses. Huge drifts of dust like sand dunes appeared and then disappeared as the wind whipped them into a different location.

(continued)

A Page from the Past

The Dust Bowl *(continued)*

Thousands of people left the Plains during the Dust Bowl. Over 300,000 of them went to California, where they hoped to find work. These migrants were called Okies. The most famous book about them is John Steinbeck's *The Grapes of Wrath*, published in 1939. A movie of the same title was made the following year and is a classic of American filmmaking. Steinbeck won a Pulitzer Prize for his novel, and John Ford won an Oscar for Best Director for his film.

What caused the Dust Bowl? Many at the time liked to blame nature and saw themselves as the innocent victims of this disaster. Today, most scientists believe that both people and nature were to blame. Poor farming techniques and a get-rich-quick attitude on the part of many produced conditions that would become disastrous when a cycle of drought hit the plains. Drought cycles always occur at some time in this area, so disaster was predictable. Today, farmers know that the ways of humans, not nature, must be changed. Thanks to improved farming and conservation techniques, the Plains are unlikely to experience another Dust Bowl like that of the 1930's.

The West in Popular Culture

Entire books have been written about this topic, and it is one with many possibilities for class discussion and further study. The Student Information Sheet provides an overview or starting point for your class. The new scholarship in western history, involving such historians as Patricia Nelson Limerick, Richard White, and Donald Worster, is important to know. It cuts through the misconceptions that popular culture engenders about the past. The Teacher's Bibliography at the end of this text will help you select some of the best new books on this subject.

Keep in mind that the entire history of the American West is currently undergoing great scrutiny, and new books are appearing quite regularly. Due to this renewal of interest in the West, this is an exciting time to be studying the westward expansion in your classes.

Preparation for This Unit: You might wish to bring up the concept of myth in dealing with the American West. Every country has a national myth, whether it be the Arthurian legends of England, the Norse sagas of the Scandinavian countries, or even the *Aeneid* of ancient Rome. You might ask the class to list our American myths and legends (e.g., Paul Bunyan, Davy Crockett, Pecos Bill) and see how many of them are connected with the western expansion. Another activity that might prove fun would be to have students compile a list of traditional American songs they are familiar with. How many are related to the West?

Student Activities: This unit ends with a culminating activity that you could use to evaluate students' understanding of the entire subject of the westward expansion. Students are asked to design a museum display on the American West. This would be appropriate as individual or group work. If you have classroom space and art supplies available, you might wish to have students construct or simulate an actual museum display. This activity is based on Howard Gardner's theory of multiple intelligences. Because it is not the traditional exam or essay assignment, it provides a good alternative assessment for students with unique skills and talents. Students with artistic skills may wish to illustrate their displays with their own original artwork rather than duplicate or reproduce photos and paintings. Students with acting skills might wish to perform the role of costumed historical interpreters to guide visitors through the museum. You could also make this activity a performance assessment by requiring students to act as "docents," or museum educators, and guide other students through the exhibits while explaining their content.

The West in Popular Culture

In 1887, William Cody, better known as Buffalo Bill, gave a royal performance of his Wild West Show in front of Queen Victoria in England. The troupe went on to tour western Europe. Cody's show confirmed for Europeans that all of America was populated by cowboys, Indians, and bucking broncos. Even today, according to historian William Goetzmann, the two most recognized symbols of the United States around the world are Mickey Mouse and the cowboy. Exchange students visiting the United States head for the malls to buy blue jeans and cowboy hats—even if they are only in the western suburbs of Boston, only ten miles west of the Atlantic coast. To most people in the United States and the world beyond, the West is an integral part of the American national identity.

The western frontier in popular culture can best be described as the West of illusion. It's the West that people hold in their imaginations. This West is not necessarily the real West as it existed in the past or exists today. Literature, movies, paintings, and television programs have projected certain images of the West that many readers or viewers accept as true. The West of the media, both print and image, provided Americans with a national myth.

The West in Literature

Why did the West became such a source of myth-making? One reason is that the western expansion happened at the same time as mass media were being developed. Dime novels, penny newspapers, and tabloid-type magazines like the *Illustrated Police News* were becoming popular just as the West was being settled. The vast new area was portrayed as the Wild West, totally different from the world east of the Mississippi River. Tales of mountain men, outlaws, Indian massacres, and cowboys drew audiences just as some people today are fascinated by lurid murder trials and talk shows.

William F. Cody was a scout for the western army. A writer using the pen name of Ned Buntline developed him into a folk hero, "Buffalo Bill." Cody became the subject of dozens of novels. These tales followed him through many different adventures, most of which he never actually participated in. These so-called dime novels were like the superhero comic books of today. Many other writers drew on the western theme. They developed series of books with the "good-guy" hero often pitted against outlaws and Indians, who became the traditional "bad guys." Zane Grey was a novelist whose books set the tone for the typical western plot: A disillusioned easterner comes to the West to find himself and is pushed by the environment to develop his finest qualities. In the 1920's, magazines took over much of the dime novel market. Short stories about the West, including those of Zane Grey, were popular with readers.

The West on Stage

Writers weren't the only people who recognized the entertainment value of the West. In 1883, Buffalo Bill Cody started his Wild West and Congress of Rough Riders Show, building on his dime novel popularity. The show featured such events as trick riding and sharpshooting. It also reenacted actual historical events such as Custer's defeat at Little Bighorn and the attack on the Deadwood stagecoach.

(continued)

The West in Popular Culture *(continued)*

> Some writers did approach the west with more realism. Willa Cather's novels *O Pioneers!* (1913) and *My Ántonia* (1918) portrayed the struggles of women settling the frontier. In the post-World War II market, Louis L'Amour's 80 western novels became best-sellers. L'Amour showed sensitivity toward Native Americans and Hispanic Americans in his novels. He is often considered the father of "modern" westerns. Western novels continue to be very popular. Larry McMurtry's book *Lonesome Dove* (1985) was not only a huge best-seller but also was made into a very popular television mini-series.

Sharpshooter Annie Oakley was a big hit with European audiences. She was raised in Ohio and never had been west until she joined the Wild West Show. Cody hired Native Americans for his show and staged elaborate pageants of cowboys and Indians. Several other touring Wild West shows gave easterners a thrilling look at the West of their dreams at the turn of the century. All this built up the myth of the West, both at home and abroad.

The West in Motion Pictures

By the second decade of the twentieth century, the popularity of the Wild West Show was fading. A new entertainment medium was becoming very popular—the motion picture. From their very beginning, movies used the West as a major theme.

> One of the earliest hit films was *The Great Train Robbery*, made in 1903 for Thomas Edison's Biograph Company. The director, Edwin S. Porter, shot the scenes in Dover, New Jersey. One of the actors kept falling off his horse because he didn't know how to ride. (Ironically, he later went on to become the first great star of western films, Bronco Billy.) *The Great Train Robbery* was an action picture with a chase scene, which became a classic feature of most Westerns. At the end of the film, one of the bandits faced the camera and shot his pistol right at the audience. Women fainted and men gasped in horror. Motion pictures were so new that this action was terrifying in its realism.

Movies about the West became known as westerns. They were always popular with audiences. A series of actors made their fortunes starring in westerns—William S. Hart, Tom Mix, Gary Cooper, and Clint Eastwood, to name a few. No one was more associated with the American western, though, than John Wayne. His films were easily understood and had a clear set of values. John Wayne gave the world the view that the true cowboy was decent, honorable, and brave.

(continued)

The West in Popular Culture *(continued)*

The Kobal Collection

Tom Mix, shown here in 1920, was one of the actors who starred in westerns.

Was the West that was depicted in the movies historically accurate? Usually not.

People didn't go to the movies for a history lesson, but to be entertained. Film historian Kevin Brownlow asked a former cowboy the difference between the West of motion pictures and the West as he had known it. The cowboy answered with another question: "What's the difference between daylight and dark?" The Hollywood western helped to perpetuate the myth of the West. Film cowboys were always white Anglo-Americans, women were usually refined and retiring, and most Indians were the enemy.

The West on Television

The western was popular not only on the big screen, but also on the small personal screen of television. Between 1947 and 1960, dozens of western shows were on TV. These included *The Lone Ranger, Hopalong Cassidy, The Roy Rogers Show*, and one of the longest-running series in the history of TV, *Gunsmoke*. After 1960, the western faded in popularity for series television. Western films on the many cable movie channels, though, continue to entertain large numbers of people.

Two recent movies provided a different picture of the West: *Dances with Wolves* (1990) and *The Unforgiven* (1992). Both movies won Academy Awards for Best Picture as well as many other Oscars. In *Dances with Wolves*, the Native Americans were the civilized people of the Plains. The whites were the despoilers of the environment. In the film, the Indians spoke the Lakota language rather than unintelligible grunts and single-syllable English as in movies of the past.

(continued)

The West in Popular Culture (continued)

The West in Art

The West as shown in Hollywood movies was, of course, recreated for the camera. What about paintings of the West done by artists from real life? Weren't they accurate representations? Certainly, one would think so. Artists went along with surveying parties to record what the scientists and mapmakers were studying. Very often, these artists let the landscapes of the West overcome their sense of realism. Many paintings became romanticized scenes of the West, bearing little resemblance to the actual landscape. For example, Albert Bierstadt painted "A Storm in the Rockies—Mt. Rosalie" in 1866. It was a dramatic painting, but Mt. Rosalie didn't exist. Bierstadt named the imaginary mountain after his wife. The paintings of Frederic Remington also perpetuated the myth of the "wild, wild" West. Remington's subjects revolved around Indian attacks and cowboys.

In the 1860's and 1870's, cameras had become portable enough so that photography could be used extensively in the West. Accurate pictures could be made of the landscale and people. Yet even photographers could be selective, taking only those shots that would most interest an audience.

National Cowboy Hall of Fame Collection, Oklahoma City, Oklahoma

This oil painting by Albert Bierstadt is entitled *Emigrants Crossing the Plains,* 1867.

(continued)

The West in Popular Culture *(continued)*

The West Remembered

For most people the West is still a place that seems bigger than life, a land of opportunity and adventure. An organization called Shadows of the Past enables people to reenact the Old West. Group members research an actual historical character of the past. Then they attempt to "become" that character through role-playing. It can cost as much as $1,000 to outfit yourself correctly. Another nationwide organization, called Westerners, is a club for people who love the history and lore of the American West. A local club is called a "corral" or "posse." The club president is the "sheriff." People who participate in reenacting and western clubs feel it is a way to connect with the past and attempt to understand how people lived then.

The West will probably continue to exist in our minds in two forms. There is the West of dreams and myths, a place of idealized adventure. It is important to remember, though, that there is also a much more complex West populated by a diverse group of people. This West has seen success as well as failure, abundance but also scarcity. It is a land of great beauty but also of ecological disaster and blight. Some people did move into the frontier of the West from the East along trails in covered wagons. But people also moved into the West from across the Pacific Ocean and northward from Mexico. Migration and immigration into the West continues today from many sources.

The West in our popular culture and as part of our national myth continues to entertain. In order to truly understand the West, though, we must cut through the myth and expand our knowledge. The story of the American people heading west is an important part of our national history. In reality it is a more rich and complex story than the myth perpetuated in our popular culture.

Heading West—The Final Challenge

You have been hired to design a room in a new museum of American history. The title of this room is "The American West—Yesterday and Today." The room is 25 feet by 25 feet with a center room divider that is 10 feet long. Display cases line the walls. You may also use free-standing displays on the floor space. Remember, though, to leave room for people to move through the exhibit area. A floor plan of your room is provided below. The wall displays should cover these topics: "The West 1820–1840," "The West 1840–1860," "The West 1860–1890," and "The West in Popular Culture Today." You may choose the subject for the display on the center room divider.

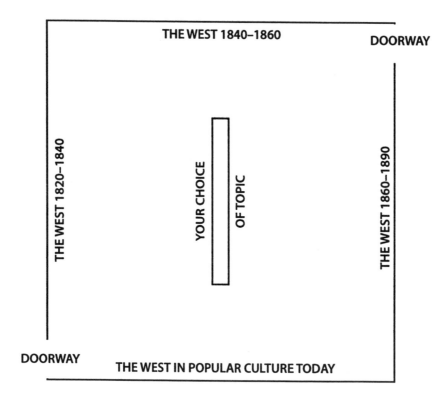

What will you display on each wall? What photographs will you use? (Remember that photography really wasn't used until the 1850's.) What paintings will you display? what maps? diagrams? You should also display artifacts—human-made objects from the specific time period. In the spaces provided on the next three pages, list your choices. You should think about what would make your displays visually appealing and of interest to your audience, the museum-goer. The displays must also be historically accurate!

(continued)

Heading West—The Final Challenge *(continued)*

The West 1820–1840

photos/paintings

_____

_____

_____

_____

maps/diagrams

_____

_____

_____

artifacts

_____

_____

_____

_____

other ideas?

_____

_____

_____

_____

The West 1840–1860

photos/paintings

_____

_____

_____

_____

maps/diagrams

_____

_____

_____

artifacts

_____

_____

_____

_____

other ideas?

_____

_____

_____

_____

(continued)

Heading West—The Final Challenge *(continued)*

The West 1860–1890

photos/paintings

_____

_____

_____

_____

maps/diagrams

_____

_____

_____

artifacts

_____

_____

_____

_____

other ideas?

_____

_____

_____

The West in Popular Culture Today

photos/paintings

_____

_____

_____

_____

maps/diagrams

_____

_____

_____

artifacts

_____

_____

_____

_____

other ideas?

_____

_____

_____

(continued)

Heading West

Heading West—The Final Challenge *(continued)*

Center Divider

Topic: _____

photos/paintings

_____

_____

_____

maps/diagrams

_____

_____

_____

artifacts

_____

_____

_____

other ideas?

_____

_____

Free-Standing Displays

_____

_____

_____

_____

artifacts

_____

_____

_____

other ideas?

_____

_____

Extra Challenge

Using 3" × 5" or 4" × 6" cards, write museum display information for the items you have chosen. You should give the title of the photo, painting, map, diagram, or artifact, who produced it, and the date. Write a paragraph explaining its significance in the history of the West during this time period.

SAMPLE: **Oil Painting:** *The Oregon Trail* (1869) by Albert Bierstadt. Bierstadt was born in Dusseldorf, Germany, but brought up in Massachusetts. He painted this wagon train after he had traveled west over the Oregon Trail. Note the oxen pulling the wagon and the emigrants driving their herds of farm animals. The entire scene is bathed in the light of the setting sun as if the golden future was in the West. Paintings such as this romanticized the journey to the West.

A Page from the Past

Early Hollywood—The Motion Picture Industry Heads West

In the early years of the twentieth century, movies were becoming big business. Films with a western theme were extremely popular with both American and European audiences. The film industry began on the East Coast. Pioneers like Thomas Edison led the way with his Biograph Company. When an early western was shot, the location was usually the Catskill Mountains or Saranac Lake, New York. The gorges at Ithaca, New York, on Lake Cayuga provided scenes for adventure films involving cliff-hanging suspense.

These "eastern" westerns looked so little like the American West that very often they were not shown to western audiences. One Pathé film titled *A Western Hero* (1909) featured Indians wearing gingham shirts and cowboys riding on English saddles. They galloped down paved roads chasing a horse-drawn omnibus instead of a stagecoach. European audiences were not too critical of these errors. Many U.S. viewers, though, found the gross inaccuracies embarrassing.

The financial incentive to turn out as many films as possible, plus the popularity of Westerns, led several early filmmakers to head to California. The Los Angeles Chamber of Commerce boasted that its city had 350 days of sunshine a year. This appealed to moviemakers who wanted a shooting schedule that would not be interrupted by bad weather. In the West, the movie industry found a bonus: scenery that was authentic for their westerns.

Some movie companies headed West for another reason. They wanted to be as far from

Thomas Edison's New Jersey as possible. Edison had formed many movie companies into a huge "movie trust" that paid royalties to use Edison's patented cameras and equipment. Many independent filmmakers violated these patents. They headed West to escape lawsuits brought against them by Edison's trust. The trust used more than lawsuits to force compliance. It often employed gangsters to threaten the independents. Gunmen would sometimes shoot a hole in a patent-breaker's camera. In California, independent filmmakers were able to hide out in remote locations. They also hired cowboys to act as lookouts and bodyguards.

By 1912, the largest concentration of motion picture companies in the United States was clustered in the Los Angeles area, particularly in a small village called Hollywood. By 1929, motion picture-making was the top industry in California, employing 100,000 people.

In the early Hollywood movies, real cowboys were very often employed as extras. This gave them a chance to earn a living in the new, modern West from which their original jobs were disappearing. Rodeo stars also were in demand. Performers in the Wild West shows often made the transition from live performances to the movies. The famous lawman Wyatt Earp visited the sets of movies in his old age. He tried to persuade directors to make the story of his life. He also tried acting, but he wasn't good enough to appear in films.

(continued)

A Page from the Past

Early Hollywood *(continued)*

Many of the big western films stars were not true cowboys, but were born in the East. William S. Hart started his career as a stage actor in New York. He became so much a symbol of the West that real cowboys loved him and rarely criticized him for being unauthentic. Tom Mix made up an elaborate story about his life before films. He claimed he was born in a log cabin in El Paso. He said he was a veteran of the Spanish-American War, the Boxer Rebellion in China, and the Boer War in Africa. He had been a lumberjack, a sheriff, and a Texas Ranger, he stated. In reality, he had been born in Pennsylvania, enlisted in the U.S. army, and then deserted. He got most of his experience working in rodeos and Wild West shows.

Mix was responsible for setting the standard costume for the movie cowboy. As time went on, his outfits got more elaborate. He dressed in satin shirts, a white hat, and hand-tooled boots. Later movie cowboys emulated Mix with their fancy dress, not the sort of clothing you would ever see on a working cowboy. As well known as Mix was his sidekick horse, Tony. Other movie cowboys copied Mix on this score too, having a horse with which they were identified. Roy Rogers and Trigger and Gene Autry and Champion were screen part-nerships recognized by millions of American children.

Moving Through the Frontier of the Web: Researching the Westward Movement on the Internet

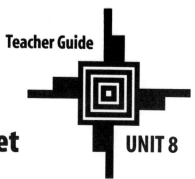

In a letter to the *Boston Globe* dated June 6, 1996, an irate writer stated that the Internet had absolutely no place in schools and was a great waste of time. The writer had futilely spent two weeks trying to use the Net. All the more reason for teachers to educate their students on how to use the Internet and its resources correctly! We teach students to evaluate and be selective about library materials. We also must teach students how to evaluate Web resources and avoid the abundant cyber-garbage. The skill of separating the useful information from the trivial promotes lifelong learning.

In researching the World Wide Web, it is helpful (if not essential) to have some sort of Web browser like Netscape, which can connect you easily to the different search engines like Yahoo, Webcrawler, Lycos, or Alta Vista. Using these search services, you can often simply type in key words like "western frontier" and get some interesting results. Lycos, for example, gives you a synopsis of the site, while Webcrawler simply gives you the site's title. A small sample of some Web sites from a search of "western frontier":

- a history of African American cavalry soldiers in the West;

- a chapter of a book on the frontier by Henry Nash Smith;

- a syllabus for a course on the frontier from Colorado State University, which included a book list.

Although much Web information is commercially oriented—product information, buyer's guides, etc.—even corporate Web pages can provide educational resources. Wells Fargo Bank in San Francisco, for example, has a company history of their stagecoach lines and addresses of their museums. Here are a few Web addresses to get you started:

- Companion web site to the PBS series http://www3.pbs.org/weta/thewest

- Endangered species of animals and plants; has maps and lists of species by region: http://www.nceet.snre.umich.edu/ EndSpp/Endangered.html

- Environmental education lesson plans: Gopher nceet.snre.umich.edu

- Mormons and the history of the Mormon Church: http://www.teleport.com/~ldsinfo/ index.html

- Motion pictures—database of over 39,000 movies with reviews and credits: http://www. msstate.edu/Movies/

- Native Americans—list of federally recognized tribes with links to their pages: http://www.afn.org/~native/tribesl.htm

- Primary documents in U.S. history, all in full text (the University of Kansas has lots of history resources): http://history.cc.ukans.edu/carrie/docs/docs_us.html

- or try— http://history.cc.ukans.edu/history/www_history_main.html

- Kathy Schrock is a teacher on Cape Cod, Massachusetts, who has compiled an excellent list of educational resources for teachers: http://www.capecod.net/Wixon/Wixon.htm

- Ellen Berne is a librarian at the Winsor School in Boston; she has compiled a Ready Reference Guide for teachers which is a collection of links arranged by subject heading: http://k12.oit.umass.edu/rref.html

- This site has links to gifted and talented resources: http://www.eskimo.com/~user/kids.html

- Tour the Smithsonian Institution: http://www.si.edu

- This site has full-text information on environmental issues: http://www.envirolink.org/elib/issues/issues/

- Activities based on environmental issues for grades K–12: http://www.nceet.snre.umich.edu/

- Information about the Oregon Trail, including lesson ideas: http://www.isu.edu/~trinmich/oregontrail.html

- History of Wells Fargo stagecoach company; has some fun adventure stories: http://wellsfargo.com/ftr/ftrsty

- A detailed guide to the prairie as an important ecosystem: http://www. prairienet.org/community/clubs/gpf/homepage.html

- The history and importance of the American bison; very complete: http://www.ilhawaii.net/~stony/buffalo.html

- The Levi Strauss Company has some history on their page; students can call or e-mail for a "Student Pack" if they wish to write a report: http://www. Levi.com

- This site has many links to American history resources: http://rowlf.cc.wwu.edu:8080/~jay/pages/america.html

- For immigration history resources: http://www.turner.com/tesi/html/migration.html

- The Jefferson Expansion Memorial is a wonderful museum at the base of the arch in St. Louis. It covers the period of westward expansion from the Lewis and Clark expedition on through the 19th century: http://www.st-louis.mo.us/st-louis/arch

- Kids love horses, and the animals were an important force in the westward expansion. This site is from the International Museum of the Horse and has great history resources, including a section on the buffalo soldiers, African-Americans in the cavalary:
  http://www.horseworld.com/imh/imhmain.html

- Good social studies site, has great links and pictures of the railroads and land rushes:
  http://www.indirect.com/www/dhixson/soc.html

- Many American Experience programs dealt with the westward expansion; here is how to get information about videos and how to order them:
  http://www.boston.com/wgbh/americanexperience

- The Shadows of the Past, an Old West historical reenactment group has a home page with some good information about the West, particularly films and film resources:
  http://www.sptddog.com/sotp.html

Bibliography

This list of resources is by no means inclusive. Many materials are available to teach about the westward expansion. The materials in this bibliography are listed due to their availability, particular subject matter, or outstanding bibliographies to lead the teacher to further research. Books specifically about Native Americans are not included in this list, but most sources have bibliographies with American Indian materials listed. Many of these books are also appropriate for student research. Books designated with an asterisk (*) are particularly appropriate for students. *American Heritage*, *National Geographic*, and *Smithsonian* magazines are excellent sources for the westward expansion with good illustrations and photographs.

General Books on the Westward Expansion

The Jefferson Expansion National Historical Association has a wonderful book and video catalog of American western history called "Gone West!" that includes many of these resources. Their toll-free number is 1-800-537-7962. Their address is 11 North Fourth Street, St. Louis, MO 63102. Proceeds from sales generate donations to the National Park Service programs.

Billington, Ray Allen. *The Far Western Frontier, 1830-1860.* New York: Harper & Row, 1956. Has a good chronology of events for those years.*

Billington, Ray Allen, and Martin Ridge. *Westward Expansion: A History of the American Frontier.* New York: Macmillan, 1967. The traditional textbook on the westward movement. Has been recently criticized for its traditional approach.*

DeVoto, Bernard. *The Year of Decision: 1846.* Boston: Houghton Mifflin, 1942. A classic. DeVoto presumes quite a bit of knowledge about American history, but he writes in a literary, entertaining style.

Flanagan, Mike. *The Old West Day by Day.* New York: Facts on File, 1995. A fun book for students and teachers alike. It gives day-by-day events as well as information about important individuals for each year in western history.*

Foote, Timothy. "1846, The Way We Were—and the Way We Went," *Smithsonian*, April 1996. Good synopsis of the initial push to the Far West.*

Lamar, Howard R., ed. *The Reader's Encyclopedia of the American West.* New York: Crowell, 1977. An excellent reference book, but students must know what they are looking for. Not for idle browsing.*

Lavender, David. *The American Heritage History of the Great West*. New York: American Heritage, 1982. Starts with America's colonial past and the push across the Appalachians and ends with the early 1920's. Good illustrations.*

Limerick, Patricia Nelson, Clyde A. Milner II, and Charles E. Rankin, eds. *Trails: Towards a New Western History*. Lawrence, KS: University of Kansas Press, 1991. An intellectually stimulating look at the new scholarship of western history.

Milner, Clyde A. II, Carol A. O'Connor, and Martha A. Sandweiss, eds. *The Oxford History of the American West*. New York: Oxford University Press, 1994. A very inclusive book with much information. Highly recommended for any school library.*

Time-Life Books, ed. *The Wild West*. New York: Warner Books, 1993. A colorful, lavishly illustrated book that will appeal to students. Based on a TV miniseries.*

Ward, Geoffrey C. *The West*. Boston: Little Brown Co., 1996. The companion volume to the PBS series of the same name.*

White, Richard. *"It's Your Misfortune and None of My Own": A History of the American West*. Norman, OK: University of Oklahoma Press, 1991. Combines the best of the new scholarship on the West with the traditional topics. Highly recommended.*

The National Park Service has a series of excellent booklets about the historic sites connected with the westward expansion, such as Fort Laramie and the Oregon Trail. They can be ordered by contacting the Superintendent of Documents, U.S. Government Printing Office, Washington, DC 20402. Many booklets can be purchased at National Historic sites and parks.

Unit 1: The Concept of the Frontier: A Background Study of the Westward Expansion

Billington, Ray Allen. *America's Frontier Heritage*. New York: Holt, Rinehart, Winston, 1961. Billington is one of the foremost western historians, although his work has been criticized by the "new" western historians as not being inclusive.

Billington, Ray Allen. "How the Frontier Shaped the American Character," *American Heritage*, Vol. IX, No. 3 (April 1958), pp. 4–9+. Good synopsis of Turner's Frontier Thesis.*

Cummins, D. Duane, and William Gee White. *The American Frontier*. New York: Benziger Brothers, 1968. Very basic, but a good introduction to the concept of the frontier and the push west.*

Limerick, Patricia Nelson. *The Legacy of Conquest: The Unbroken Past of the American West*. W.W. Norton, 1987. Limerick is viewed as one of the most influential new scholars on the West. This is a thought-provoking look at many issues in western history.

Turner, Frederick Jackson. "The Significance of the Frontier in American History." Several reprints of this famous paper, given to the American Historical Association in 1893, are available. Despite recent debunking, this work is an excellent lesson in historiography.

Unit 2: *Reasons for the Move West*

Katz, William Loren. *The Black West.* NY: Doubleday, Garden City, 1971. A good overview about black pioneers.*

Libo, Kenneth, and Irving Howe. *We Lived There Too.* New York: St. Martin's Press, 1984. A look at Jewish pioneers and the westward movement from 1630 to 1930. Contains excellent primary sources and illustrations.*

Stegner, Wallace. *The Gathering of Zion.* New York: McGraw-Hill, 1964. Classic history of the Mormon emigration to the Salt Lake Basin.*

Unit 3: *Finding a Route*
and
Unit 4: *Moving West*

Franzwa, Gregory M. *The Oregon Trail Revisited.* Tucson, AZ: Patrice Press, 1988.*

Stewart, George R. *Ordeal By Hunger.* Boston: Houghton Mifflin, 1936. Best-known work about the ill-fated Donner Party.*

Unruh, John D., Jr. *The Plains Across: The Overland Emigrants and the Trans-Mississippi West, 1840-1860.* Urbana, IL: University of Illinois Press, 1979. A classic work on the migration west via the overland trails.

Unit 5: *Selling the West: The Lure of Land and Truth in Advertising*

Frazier, Ian. *Great Plains.* New York: Farrar, Strauss, Giroux, 1989. Frazier makes a modern trip across the Plains and looks at our past and future. A wonderful, insightful book.*

Schlissel, Lillian. *Women's Diaries of the Westward Journey.* New York: Schocken, 1982. Contains good primary sources and certainly dispels the myth of women being frail. Good view of the realities facing settlers.*

Unit 6: *The Environmental Impact of the Migration Westward*

Chadwick, Douglas. "The American Prairie." *National Geographic,* Vol. 184, No. 4, (October 1993), pp. 90-119. Excellent look at the prairie ecosystem.*

Hodgson, Bryan. "Buffalo: Back Home on the Range." *National Geographic,* Vol. 186, No. 5, (November 1994), pp. 64-89. Looks at the history of the bison and its comeback thanks to conservation and private enterprise.*

Naar, Jon, and Alex J. Naar. *This Land Is Your Land.* New York: HarperCollins, 1993. Divides the United States into ecosystems and examines the danger to each. Also contains a section on what private citizens can do to affect change, lists of organizations, and bibliographies for further reading.*

Worster, Donald. *Under Western Skies: Nature and History in the American West.* New York: Oxford University Press, 1992. One of the best new books dealing with environmental issues in the West.

Zwingle, Erla. "Wellspring of the High Plains." *National Geographic,* Vol. 183, No. 3, (March 1993), pp. 80-109. Excellent article about the Ogallalah aquifer and its depletion.

Unit 7: The West in Popular Culture

Brownlow, Kevin. *The War, The West, and The Wilderness.* New York: Alfred A. Knopf, 1979. One of the best books covering the early period of Hollywood motion pictures and the beginnings of westerns.

Goetzmann, William H., and William N. Goetzmann. *The West of the Imagination.* New York: W.W. Norton, 1986. Based on the PBS series of the same name, this is a beautifully illustrated book.*

Kowalewski, Michael, ed. *Reading the West: New Essays on the Literature of the American West.* New York: Cambridge University Press, 1996.

Smith, Henry Nash. *Virgin Land: The American West as Symbol and Myth.* Cambridge, MA: Harvard University Press, 1970. First published in 1950, this book is acknowledged as one of the first to de-bunk the myth of the frontier.

Truettner, William H., ed. *The West as America: Reinterpreting Images of the Frontier, 1820-1920.* Smithsonian Institution Press, Washington, 1991. Contains some unusual representations of the West by artists.*

Tuska, Jon. *The Filming of the West.* New York: Doubleday, 1976. Contains

wonderful photos as well as titles and sources for westerns.

Wilson, Wendy S. and Gerald H. Herman. *American History on the Screen: A Teacher's Resource Book on Film and Video.* Portland, ME: J. Weston Walch, Publisher, 1994. Has units with lessons on *The Grapes of Wrath* and *Dances With Wolves* as well as other suggestions for using feature films in American history class.

A Page from the Past

For information about the Amana Colonies, including educational materials, contact Amana Colonies Convention and Visitors Bureau, P.O. Box 303, 39-38th Avenue, Amana, IA 52203 (1-800-245-5465).

Painter, Nell Irvine. *Exodusters: Black Migration to Kansas After Reconstruction.* New York: W.W. Norton, 1976.

Klinkenborg, Verlyn. "If It Weren't for the Ox, We Wouldn't Be Where We Are." *Smithsonian Magazine,* Vol. 24, No. 6, (September 1993), pp. 82-93. Good synopsis of the importance of this animal throughout history.*

Rochlin, Harriet and Fred. *Pioneer Jews: A New Life in the Far West.* Boston: Houghton Mifflin, 1984. Contains a good summary of the life of Levi Strauss.*

Parfit, Michael. "The Dust Bowl." *Smithsonian.* Vol. 20, No. 3 (June 1989), pp. 44-57. Entertaining article based on people who remember the Dust Bowl and lived through it.*

Worster, Donald. *Dust Bowl: The South Plains in the 1930's.* New York: Oxford

University Press, New York, 1979. Worster is a noted Western environmental historian who was raised in California. His parents moved there to escape the Dust Bowl.

Media Resources

This list is based on ease of purchase and availability. Many items come with lesson plans, and all companies listed will take purchase orders.

Battle for the Plains and *The Mysterious Black-Footed Ferret*. PBS National Audubon Society specials about the ecology of the Great Media Resources for Heading West: Plains. Each video contains a teacher's guide. PBS Video, 1320 Braddock Place, Alexandria, VA 22314 (1-800-344-3337).

Buffalo Bill's Wild West Show. 45 minutes. Uses actual footage to show the West that Americans accepted as real. Available from the Jefferson Expansion National Historical Association, 11 North Fourth St., St. Louis, MO 63102 (1-800-537-7962).

The Buffalo Soldiers. 47 minutes. Story of African-American soldiers in the West. Bill Armstrong Productions. Available from the Jefferson Expansion National Historical Association, 11 North Fourth St., St. Louis, MO 63102 (1-800-537-7962).

The Donner Party. 90 minutes. A very well-done film about a gruesome chapter in the westward migration. Lesson plans outline available. PBS Video, 1320 Braddock Place, Alexandria, VA 22314 (1-800-344-3337).

In Search of the Oregon Trail. 3-hour documentary as seen on PBS. Highly recom-mended. Dispels old myths about the emigration and contains some of the best new scholarship about the West. Available for purchase by schools from Great Plains National, P.O. Box 80669, Lincoln, NE 68501-0669 (1-800-228-4630).

The Iron Road. The story of the completion of the transcontinental railroad. Includes a lesson plan outline. PBS Video, 1320 Braddock Place, Alexandria, VA 22314 (1-800-344-3337).

The Oregon Trail. 2-hour documentary shown on some PBS stations. Fairly simplistic, might be good for younger students. Can be ordered by calling 1-800-247-6553. Purchase orders accepted at Boettchner/Tricklein, 1281 N. Foothill Rd., Idaho Falls, ID 83401.

The Plow That Broke the Plains. 1936, 26 minutes. Famous documentary by Pare Lorentz sponsored by the New Deal's Resettlement Administration. A good source for this documentary is *Image as Artifact*. a video or laser disk package from the American Historical Association, 400 A Street SE, Washington, DC 20003. This compilation also contains a wonderful early D.W. Griffith film, *A Corner in Wheat*, which deals with the subject of speculation in the wheat market.

The Way West. Ric Burns's four-part series about the clash between settlers, and Native Americans. Available as a series or as individual videos. PBS Video, 1320 Braddock Place, Alexandria, VA 22314 (1-800-344-3337).

The West. Ken Burns presents a film by Stephen Ives. Eight hours. Very inclusive history of the West using the new scholarship. Available with educational materials from PBS Video, 1320 Braddock

Place, Alexandria, VA 22314
(1-800-344-3337).

The Wild West. TV miniseries about the West from the end of the Civil War to 1900. Available from Warner Home Video, (1-818-954-6000), or from Social Studies School Service, 10200 Jefferson Boulevard, Room CD3, P.O. Box 802, Culver City, CA 90232-0802 (1-800-421-4246). Companion book available; see print resources above.

CD ROMs

America Goes West. Grades 7-12. Entire history of the westward movement. Mac only. Educorp Multimedia, 7434 Trade Street, San Diego, CA 92121 -2410 (1-800-843-9497).

American Journey: History in Your Hands. Primary source materials for DOS only. One CD-ROM is titled *Westward Expansion.* Primary Source Media, 1995. Available from Social Studies School Service, 10200 Jefferson Boulevard, Room CD3, P.O. Box 802, Culver City, CA 90232-0802, (1-800-421-4246).

The American West: Myth and Reality. The development of the media West from James Fenimore Cooper to John Wayne. MAC and DOS. Video also available (from an original filmstrip) from the Social Studies School Service, 10200 Jefferson Boulevard, Room CD3, P.O. Box 802, Culver City, CA 90232-0802 (1-800-421-4246).

History of Railroads. Includes chronologies, maps, and photographs. Available for both Mac and Windows. Educorp Multimedia, 7434 Trade Street, San Diego, CA 92121-2410 (1-800-843-9497).

The Oregon Trail II. Latest version of this well-known simulation. Mac or Windows. Grades 5–12. MECC software. Many sources for this. One is Learning Services Connection, P.O. Box 10636, Eugene, OR 97440-2636; (1-800-877-3278) (East Coast), (1-800-877-9378) (West Coast).

The Wild West. Available for Windows. Based on the television miniseries, deals with the West of 1866–1896. Jasmine Multimedia. Grades 3 and up. Forest Technologies, 514 Market Loop, Suite 103, West Dundee, IL 60118 (1-800-544-3356).

Writing Along the Oregon Trail. These disks have 45 language arts projects based on *The Oregon Trail.* Mac and DOS. Available from Social Studies School Service, 10200 Jefferson Boulevard, Room CD3, P.O. Box 802, Culver City, CA 90232-0802 (1-800-421-4246).

Annotated Bibliography for Students

Anderson, Joan. *Spanish Pioneers of the Southwest*. New York: Lodestar Books, 1989.

Among the first settlers of the American frontier were the Spanish. This book pays a visit to El Rancho de las Golondrinas, representative of Spanish settlements in the mid-18th century. Current-day photographs of this living history museum bring home the realities of early settlement life.

Blos, Joan. *Brothers of the Heart*. New York: Charles Scribner, 1985.

From an Indian woman, a disabled young boy learns many of life's lessons, including how to survive on his own. The book is set in 1800's Michigan and is a story of friendship.

Brown, Dee. *Lonesome Whistle: The Story of the First Transcontinental Railroad*. New York: Holt, 1980.

This is the story of the transcontinental railroad and the effect its construction had on the immigrants who built it, the Indians whose land was taken for it, and the investors who profited (and lost) from it. The book contains excellent illustrations and maps.

Chu, Daniel, and Bill Shawl. *Going Home to Nicodemus: The Story of an African-American Frontier Town and the Pioneers Who Settled It*. Morristown, NJ: Silver Burdett Press, 1994.

The story of the founding and settling of Nicodemus, Kansas, is told in an enjoyable and readable style. While far from its heyday population, Nicodemus still exists. An annotated bibliography accompanies the book.

Conrad, Pamela. *Prairie Visions: The Life and Times of Simon Butcher*. New York: HarperCollins, 1991.

Butcher was a real-life chronicler of the Old West. He lived in the 1800's in Nebraska and recorded in photographs and anecdotes stories of prairie life.

Duncan, Dayton. *The West: An Illustrated History for Children*. Boston: Little Brown Co., 1996. Contains an introduction by Ken Burns and Stephen Ives and basically is a companion to the PBS series, but for younger readers.

Greenberg, Judith E., and Helen Carey McKeever. *A Pioneer Woman's Memoir*. New York: Franklin Watts, 1995.

Based on the memoirs of Arabella Clemens Fulton, the authors have constructed an appealing story. Illustrations and photographs serve to highlight the text.

Greenwood, Barbara. *A Pioneer Sampler: The Daily Life of a Pioneer Family in 1840*. Boston: Houghton Mifflin, 1994.

Visit with a pioneer family and discover their way of life. This is an impressive social history of a pioneer farming family. Superb illustrations, descriptive text, and crafts instructions amplify the account.

Katz, William Loren. *Black Women of the Old West*. New York: Atheneum Books, 1995.

This book is based on real-life accounts of African-American women who helped build the American frontier. Well-researched and documented, this is a must-read book for anyone interested in women and the Old West. An annotated bibliography accompanies the book.

Kherdian, David. *Bridger: The Story of a Mountain Man.* New York: Greenwillow, 1987.

This book focuses on the years 1822 to 1824 and tells the story, in Bridger's words, of his adventures and discoveries during that time. The book also sets the geographical scene of the lands Bridger traveled through.

L'Amour, Louis. *How the West Was Won.* New York: Thorndike Press, 1988.

This well-known novel presents another perspective concerning westward expansion. It is rich in historical detail and description.

Miller, Brandon Marie. *Buffalo Gals: Women of the Old West.* Minneapolis: Lerner Publications, 1994.

Employing primary sources (journals, song, original letters), the author weaves the history of women in settling the Old West. The book is not limited to women migrating west; it includes accounts of Native American women.

Miller, Marilyn. *The Transcontinental Railroad.* Morristown, NJ: Silver Burdett, 1986.

Through the use of photographs and maps, this book tells the story of the growth and development of railroads during the 1800's is told in a captivating manner.

Murphy, Jim. *The Great Fire.* New York: Scholastic, 1995.

This award-winning book the story of the conflagration of 1871 that destroyed Chicago, vividly tells replete with telling photographs and illustrations.

Painter, Nell Irvine. *Exodusters: Black Migration to Kansas After Reconstruction.* New York: W.W. Norton, 1976.

This is an excellent examination of the migration of African-Americans in 1879. The book includes significant material on the role of African-American women.

Schlissel, Lillian. *Black Frontiers: A History of African-American Heroes in the Old West.* New York: Simon & Schuster Books, 1995.

After the Civil War, many former slaves migrated to the Old West. This book utilizes text and photography to describe that migration in a revealing manner.

Toynton, Evelyn. *Growing Up in America: 1830–1860.* Brookfield, CT: The Millbrook Press, 1995.

This is a comparative study of children growing up in pre-Civil War America. The text views children at play, work, and in school and draws comparisons among children from different sections of the country.

Van Steenwyk, Elizabeth. *Frontier Fever.* New York: Walker and Company, 1995.

This entertaining book details the treatment of diseases and injuries on the frontier. Read about homemade remedies that worked, and some that didn't, as medicine progressed during the 1800's.

Additional Assessment Activities

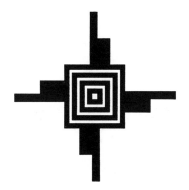

Here are some suggestions for student projects and essays you can use as a final evaluative tool.

Americans learn about the trail west through the movies, where the intrepid pioneers are always being brutally attacked by Native Americans. If this is not historically true, why is this image perpetuated?

Some historians feel that our frontier past accounts for our wastefulness as a nation and that other cultures are not as wasteful. Do you feel that this is a fair evaluation of American culture? Justify your answer with examples.

Why is the West so much a part of our popular culture? What characteristics of the westward expansion can account for the mythical quality of the West in our national history?

The West has larger urban areas than the United States east of the Mississippi. Why is this true? Does this fact clash with our traditional image of the West?

How important was the Lewis and Clark expedition in opening up the American continent to settlement?

What was the role of the fur trappers and mountain men in opening up the West?

Was the Pony Express only a romantic idea, or was it a practical solution to the problem of communication in the West?

Why was the buffalo so important for the Great Plains ecology?

What animals of the West have become extinct or endangered since 1850?

What obstacles did the builders of the transcontinental railroad face? How did they overcome these obstacles?

Describe a typical day in the life of a family traveling in a wagon train along the Oregon Trail.

African-Americans began moving west from the very beginning, when western land was first opened up. What motivated the movement of blacks into the West? What opportunities and/or problems did they face once there?

Wells Fargo was a name well known throughout the West for transportation of goods and passengers. What forms of transportation did Wells Fargo use and for what purposes?

Some historians have written that water was the key to success or failure in the West. Do you agree with this? How has water made southern California one of our most densely populated areas?

The state of medicine during the westward expansion grew progressively better during the 1800's, especially after the Civil War. What contributions did the pioneer experience provide to medical science?

Many inventions helped in the settlement of the West. Certainly, the railroad was significant. But the invention of the telegraph had a huge influence on communities and communication. Describe how the telegraph altered the westerners' way of life.

The discovery of oil, gold, silver, and other precious materials generated poor relations between American Indians and white people. What were the problems? How were they handled? Could more reasonable solutions have been found?

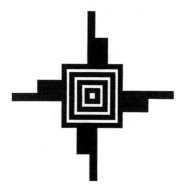

Answer Key

Unit 1: The Concept of the Frontier

Worksheet 3:
Other Frontiers—An Extra Challenge

Some helpful hints:

Russia's frontier was Siberia, the area east of the Ural Mountains. The tsarist government used Siberia as a place of exile for political dissidents and those convicted of crimes. It is an area of vast mineral and timber resources but little agriculture due to the permafrost and short growing season. The region has indigenous people much like the Inuit of our Arctic area, but they are few in number. The Soviet government in the 1960's actively encouraged people to move to Siberia and built Academic City there as a center of scholarship and technology.

Australia's frontier was the inland area known as the Outback, largely desert. The native Aborigines still inhabit areas of the Outback, but their numbers are small compared to the white settlers. Mineral wealth originally drew people into the Outback, but today it is mostly used for sheep farming where there is enough moisture.

Canada's frontier experience is closest to that of the United States. Canada had a formidable obstacle to western expansion, the Laurentian Shield, an area of unusable rocky land. The Canadian far west was first settled by fur trappers. Canada has great mineral wealth in the west and had a gold rush in 1858. The prairie provinces were settled about the same time as the United States Plains states. The Canadian transcontinental railroad was not completed until 1885. Canada's population remained small in the nineteenth century; there was little immigration until later in the twentieth century. Canada had various Native American tribes; the country seemed to have dealt with them somewhat more humanely than the United States did.

South Africa's frontier was to the north from Capetown. The Dutch settlers, known as Boers, migrated north from Capetown in the 1830's to escape British rule. They loaded their families and possessions into ox-drawn covered wagons and headed into territory controlled by a large native population of Zulus. They set up farms in territories they called the Transvaal and Orange Free State. Later, diamonds and gold was discovered in these areas. Of the four frontiers listed on the worksheet, only the South African frontier had a large population of indigenous people who always outnumbered the white settlers.

Unit 3: Finding a Route

Worksheet 2:
Geographic Obstacles to the Migration

Plains	Mountains
brush fires	mud slides
floods	poisonous snakes
poor trails	rock slides
downpours	cold
muddy trails	narrow passes
extreme temperatures	height
buffalo stampedes	no food for draft animals
	poor trails
	snow

Deserts	Rivers
quicksand	strong currents
lack of water	water depth
poisonous animals	breadth
extreme temperatures	flooding
no food for draft animals	quicksand
	lack of fuel for cooking fires

Worksheet 3: Planning the Way West

1. You need to get to one of the jumping-off places for the Oregon Trail. You would probably take a steamship to Baltimore and then go overland by stage or horseback on the National Road to Vandalia, Illinois. From Vandalia, it is not far overland to St. Louis, where you can get a riverboat to take you to Independence, Missouri. Almost as soon as the discovery of gold in California was announced, entrepreneurs set up "express" wagon trains for gold seekers. You could pick up one of these express trains at Independence or St. Joseph, Missouri. Because "49ers" tended to be single men, they could travel rather lightly and use mules either to ride or to pull simple carts. Some emigrants to California loaded their possessions on their back and walked. You would want to start your journey in the spring so as to cross the Sierra Nevadas before autumn snows hit. You would probably take the Oregon Trail to Fort Hall and then cross off on the California Trail. After the Donner Party disaster, most people avoided the Hastings Cut-off.

2. You would probably travel by riverboat up the Mississippi to the Missouri River, then on to Independence, Missouri, the traditional jumping-off site for the Oregon Trail. Riverboats commonly carried wagons, supplies, and stock as well as passengers. From there you would follow the Oregon Trail to its final destination, the Willamette Valley. You would need to start from Independence in May just as soon as the prairie grass turned green to give your oxen grass to eat and to start the journey in time to arrive in Oregon before the onset of winter.

3. Water is always the cheapest way to ship bulk goods. You would take the Lowell to Boston canal and then take a steamship to New York City and up the Hudson River to Albany. From Albany, you would take a barge on the Erie Canal to Buffalo, then a steamer on Lake Erie to Cleveland. A mule could pull a canal barge at as much as four miles per hour. Allow yourself three to four weeks for the trip to be on the safe side. You could travel anytime provided you avoid the winter months when the canal would be frozen.

4. Probably the best route for you to take would be to load up your Conestoga-type wagon and travel along the Wilderness Road to the National Road. The National Road will take you directly

into southern Illinois. Many who wished to leave the South for the Old Northwest used this route. It would be best to travel in the spring so that you might have time to get a crop in when you arrive, but some emigrants left at all times during the year, even winter.

5. You would load your supplies on a steamboat at St. Louis, including your Murphy wagons, large vehicles capable of handling several tons, and go to Independence. At Independence, you would unload, procure mules or oxen for the trip, and head toward Council Grove, 150 miles from Independence (about ten days' journey). At Council Grove, you would meet with other traders and organize a wagon train for the trip to Santa Fe along the Santa Fe Trail, a trip which took about over two months. You would start in the spring when the prairie grass became green.

6. **Extra Challenge.** The Mormons traveled the same route as the emigrants to Oregon, only they began farther to the north at Council Bluffs, Iowa, and then traveled along the north bank of the Platte River to avoid any conflict. At Fort Laramie, they rejoined the mai trail and then at Fort Bridger continued southwest to the Great Salt Lake.

Worksheet 1: Getting Prepared

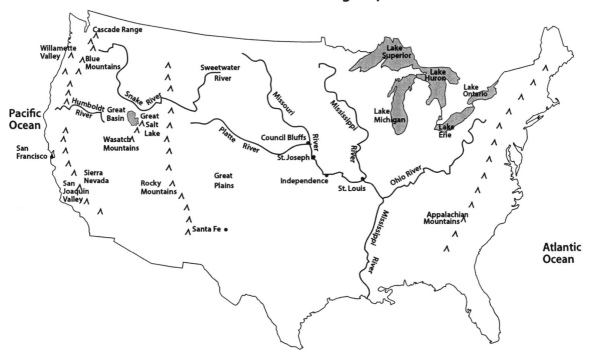

Unit 6: The Environmental Impact of the Migration Westward

Worksheet 1:
What Has Happened to Them?

The black-footed ferret depends on the prairie dog for food. Due to the poisoning of prairie dogs, the black-footed ferret disappeared from the wild in 1987. Biologists captured the last remaining ferrets and have been breeding them in captivity for release into prairie preserves.

Prairie dogs have been poisoned by farmers fear their livestock will break their legs in the prairie dogs' burrows and also because they think that prairie dogs eat all the grass needed for stock. Prairie dogs only eat about 7 percent of the grass from a particular area, but their population has declined by 90 percent due to poisoning.

The Audubon bighorn has been extinct since 1925. A subspecies of the bighorn sheep found in mountainous areas, it lived on the Plains until overhunting and diseases it caught from livestock wiped them out.

Elk can still be found in prairie areas. They are less numerous than they used to be due to hunting and loss of habitat. Many herds have moved into forest areas away from the prairies.

Sandhill cranes are an endangered species. They are migratory and depend on the Platte River wetlands to nest. Most of this wetland area has been turned into farmland. The sandhill population is being monitored by scientists and environmental groups.

Passenger pigeons were killed by settlers in such vast numbers that they became extinct. The railroads shipped the young birds (squab) to restaurants and markets in the eastern cities. The last passenger pigeon died in the Cincinnati Zoo in 1914.

About the Authors

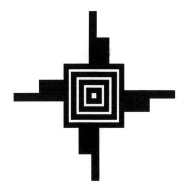

Wendy S. Wilson has been a teacher in the Lexington, Massachusetts, public schools since 1971. She has taught social studies in grades 7–12 and is also a senior lecturer in history at University College, Northeastern University. She is co-author of other Walch publications, *American History on the Screen* with Gerald H. Herman, and *Ellis Island and Beyond* with Jack Papadonis. She has done extensive consulting work in the field of history-based media productions, including the educational print materials for the PBS series *The West*.

Jack Papadonis is the K–12 social studies curriculum coordinator for the Lexington public schools. He is a member of the adjunct faculty of Lesley College and consults with school districts regarding social studies curriculum and instructional practice. He has served as president of the Massachusetts Council for the Social Studies and is a member of the National Council for the Social Studies Curriculum Committee. He is a co-founder of the History-Social Studies School-College Alliance. The purpose of the alliance, headquartered in the History Department at Northeastern University, is to enhance the teaching of social studies by providing curriculum materials and support to teachers and students.

The authors would like to thank the History Department of Northeastern University, particularly Assistant Professor Gerald H. Herman, for the support given in the research and writing of this project.